Siku Kayak

Also by Ray Jardine

Beyond Backpacking
Ray Jardine's
Guide To Lightweight Hiking

Practical methods for all who love the out-of-doors, from walkers and backpackers, to long-distance hikers

The Ray-Way Tarp Book
How to Use a Tarp in the Wilds

And how to make one at home

Net-Tent, Stowbags and PolyTarp Included

Lightweight shelters for backpackers and hikers, cyclists, sea-kayakers, canoeists, scouts, and anyone else who enjoys camping

Atlantic Caper
Rowing across the Atlantic Ocean

Video on DVD and VHS

We invite you to visit our web site
for more information about our products

www.RayJardine.com

P.O. Box 2153 Arizona City, AZ 85223

Siku Kayak

Paddling the Coast of Arctic Alaska
Ray & Jenny Jardine

Siku Kayak

Paddling the Coast of Arctic Alaska

Copyright © 2005 by Ray Jardine

Photographs and maps © Ray and Jenny Jardine

Printed and bound in the United States of America. All rights reserved. No part of this book may be reproduced in any form or by any electronic or mechanical means including information storage and retrieval systems without permission in writing from the publisher, except by a reviewer who may quote brief passages.

Although the author and publisher have exhaustively researched all sources to ensure the accuracy and completeness of the information contained here, we assume no responsibility for errors, inaccuracies, omissions, or inconsistencies.

This book is a trip narration only. It is not intended to instruct or encourage others. Sea kayaking Arctic regions can be extremely dangerous, and should not be attempted without a great deal of experience.

First Printing. Published in the United States by

AdventureLore Press

P.O. Box 2153, Arizona City, AZ 85223

www.RayJardine.com

Library of Congress Control Number: 2004112449

Ray Jardine, Siku Kayak

AdventureLore Press, Arizona City, Arizona

ISBN 0-9632359-6-6

Barrow
Wainright
Point Lay
Point Hope
Kotzebue
Shishmaref
Nome
Kaktovik
Inuvik
Alaska

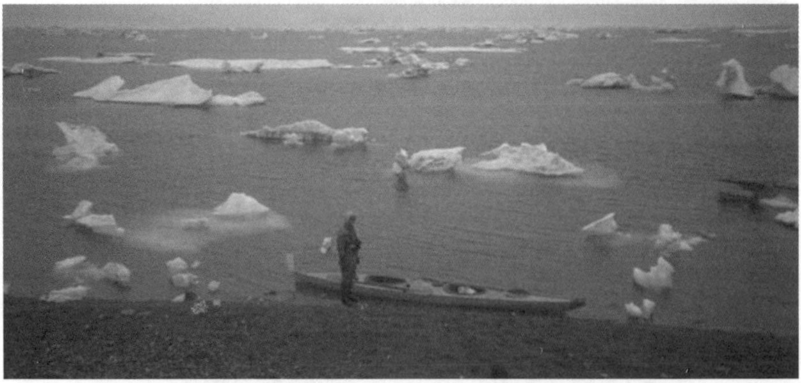

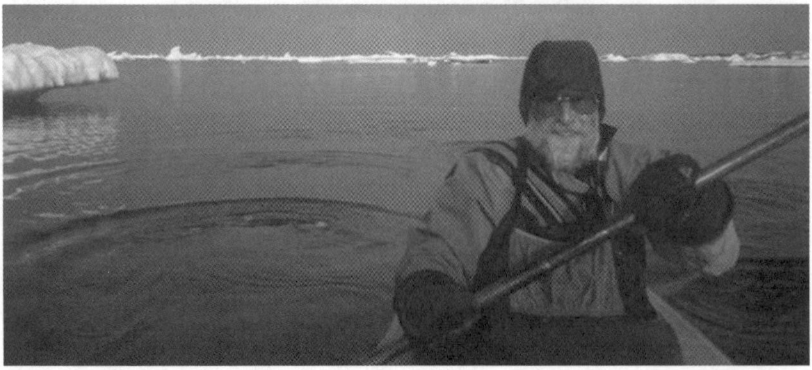

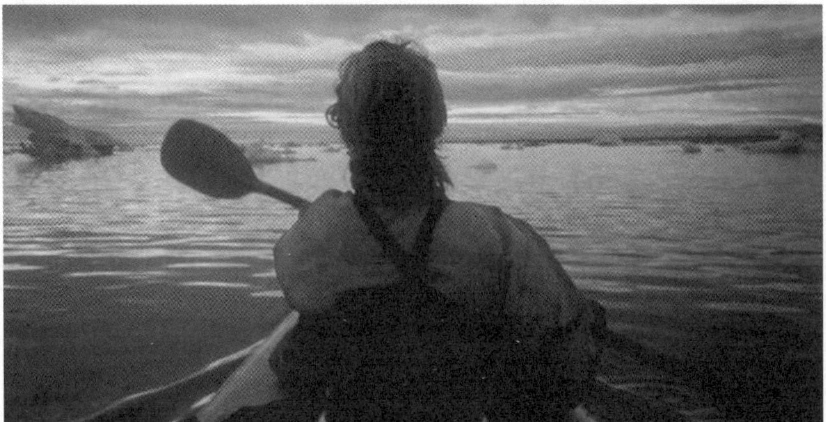

Prologue

To most sea-kayakers the Arctic is one of the least appealing destinations on earth. Its distances are vast and its solitude profound. Its seas are frigid and often choked with ice. Gales are frequent and can drop the wind-chill factor off the scales. Mosquitoes and black flies can swarm during rare periods of calm. Grizzly bears are common, and polar bears are possible. And the weather can be so volatile and unforgiving that even small mistakes could bring enormous consequences.

Yet to Jenny and me the Arctic is paradise, especially when traveling and exploring by kayak. It is relatively untouched, teeming with wildlife, and where the sky meets land there is endless and unmatched beauty. The sparkling coastlines are clean and wild, and ideal for kayak travel – at least if one has the proper skills.

These skills are unique to the Arctic, and one's kayaking experience in warmer climates does not count for much there. So the skills are best gained in intermediate regions: above the lower 48 but well below the Arctic proper.

8 -- *Siku Kayak*

In 1987 Jenny and I departed Anacortes, Washington in a two-person kayak, intent on gaining some of those intermediate-latitude skills as we progressed gradually north. That summer we paddled 1,100 miles along the western coasts of Canada and Southwest Alaska to Skagway - through a region known as the Inside Passage. After portaging the Chilkoot National Historic Trail, we followed the Yukon River 2,000 miles through the heart of Alaska to the Bering Sea.

We referred to that journey as "Saga of the Sea Tub," and in 100 days we paddled 3,392 miles.

In 1995 we decided to return to the far north. With an aerospace engineering background, I enjoy designing and building projects from scratch. So for this trip I designed the kayak with software I had written, and we built it of cored carbon-fiber and epoxy.

We flew this kayak to St. Marys, which is a hundred miles up the Yukon River from the Bering Sea. Leaving no un-paddled gap beyond our first Alaskan trip, we proceeded to the sea and continued around Norton Sound to Nome. The kayak handled beautifully, even though the weather was often extremely challenging. Continuing beyond Nome we reached the village of Shishmaref, and there called it quits – mainly because some of our clothing, and especially our tent, were proving inadequate in the unremitting storms. Even so, we managed 600 miles in 48 days. And if the distance covered was comparatively modest, at least we were gaining valuable knowledge and skills for paddling and camping in the higher latitudes. And we knew these would serve us well on future trips.

10 -- *Siku Kayak*

Keen to return to Shishmaref and continue our journey north along the Alaska coast, we spent much of the next winter preparing for the journey described in this book. We knew that if the trip were to prove successful, it would surely be one of the most interesting, challenging, and rewarding in all our experience. We also knew that it could be the most difficult and dangerous. Yet we felt we had gained the needed experience, and had developed the appropriate skills to handle the challenges unique to the Arctic.

We also knew that this next trip would require a selection of highly specialized equipment. The main problem the previous year had been our ordinary backpacking tent, so on a certain special recommendation we purchased a very expensive type. More importantly, I designed a second kayak on my computer, and we proceeded to build it in our garage, this time using kevlar, carbon fiber and epoxy.

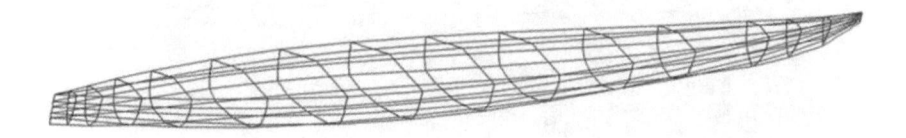

After designing the kayak on the computer, we plotted the mold frames on particleboard, cut them to size, and mounted them on a strongback, shown above. Then using an ordinary skill saw mounted on a homemade frame, we cut the mold stringers.

12 -- *Siku Kayak*

Next we attached the stringers to the frames, shown at left. At this point we were building the mold, not the actual kayak. The mold was the typical strip planked construction of the type often used to make canoes.

Photo bottom left shows the completed mold, clear-coated and painted with a non-stick compound. Nearby is a rack of kevlar cloth.

Here we have begun to build the actual kayak, draping the kevlar cloth over the mold and applying the epoxy resin. This is known as the "wet layup" method.

Once the kevlar had hardened we removed the mold. Then we laminated the kevlar with carbon fibre. This created a very strong and light hull.

An exciting day for the designer: the boat's first time in the water. Because the epoxy was still "green," only one of us could sit in it at a time.

Once we had completed the deck and fitted it to the hull, we added cockpit combings and hatch rims.

Jenny sewed custom spray skirts which bungied over the cockpit rims. The skirts are worn to keep the rain, splash and crashing waves out of the cockpits. The dog belonged to a neighbor but prefered to spend most of its time in our garage-shop overseeing the kayak building project.

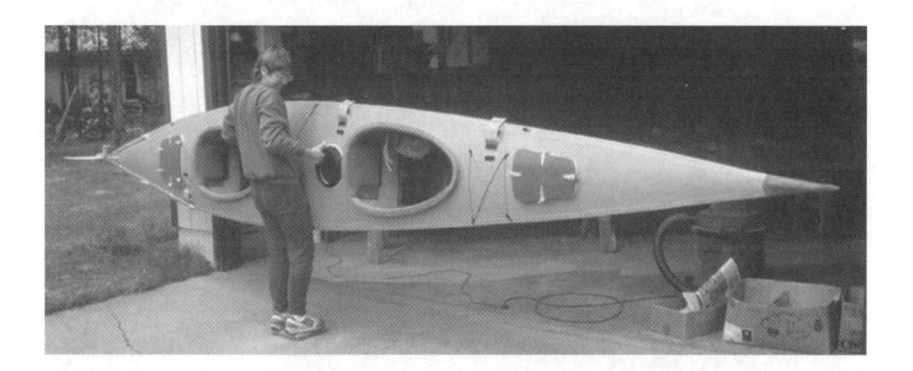

Jenny standing on the bathroom scales while holding the kayak. With a beam of 30" and a length of 19½ feet (plus 6 inches rudder), "Siku" weighed 52 pounds. This weight included the deck cored with 1/4" structural foam for added stiffness, four bulkheads, three cargo hatch covers, and the rudder and peddles.

16 -- *Siku Kayak*

Once we had basically completed the kayak, we began taking it to the local lakes for testing and physical conditioning. We also started practicing certain self-rescue measures that we developed especially for this kayak. One of us would slip out of the cockpit and into the lake. Grasping the coaming we would practice a dolphin kick maneuver. The idea was to propel ourselves up and out of the water, and onto the cockpit, belly down. Then we would simply roll into the cockpit. Initially we were not particularly graceful at this, and we imagined that a walrus looking on might have chuckled at our attempts. Graceful or not, we kept practicing, and once we had refined this method we both went into the water, and in turn re-boarded. When accomplished at that, we began rolling the boat over while seated, wet exiting, then re-entering. This worked very well, and gave us the confidence to venture into Arctic waters.

Opposite: 1) The drysuit is completely waterproof. I am wearing my normal clothing under it. 2) The dolphin kick with a slight hands pull launches me onto the cockpit. 3) Lying on the cockpit belly down, I roll into my seat. This works, in part because I had designed the boat with a 30 inch beam and a fairly fbottom, both of which lent themselves greatly to lateral stability.

Jenny helped build the boat, but mainly worked on her own important projects. She sewed spray skirts, made an absolutely excellent selection of cold-weather, expedition clothing, prepared and packaged our food into resupply boxes, and made arrangements for the kayak's transportation to Shishmaref.

Jenny's sewing handiwork included a sleeping quilt, rain parkas, shell jackets and pants, warm shirts, pants, mittens, hats and socks, and heavy-gauge nylon muklucks.

Siku Kayak -- 19

Shishmaref
Kotzebue
Alaska
Nome
Anchorage

Siku Kayak

Paddling the Coast of Arctic Alaska

1,400 miles in 79 days

Two weeks prior to departure we sent the kayak on its way north. To prepare the boat for shipping, we loaded some of our lighter gear into its compartments, then wrapped large sheets of cardboard around the boat, and finally wrapped everything with heavy plastic secured with duct tape and cords. The kayak would travel by truck to Seattle, cargo ship to Anchorage, and aircraft to Nome. If the arrangements went according to plan, the boat would arrive in Nome just a few days ahead of us.

Day 1: June 5, 1996 - Nome

After a long day of commercial travel ourselves, the early evening found us on final approach to the remote outpost of Nome, Alaska. Looking out the plane's windows we could see ominous white caps sweeping across the sea. Anchorage had been in the 70's earlier that afternoon, so deplaning into Nome's 34° F temperatures felt like stepping into a deep freeze. Except that the tempest was blowing directly from Siberia, and the icy blast had dropped the wind chill factor practically off the scales. "Welcome to our Arctic summer," we chuckled.

Nome's airport was built on an enormous gravel pan, a remnant of the gold-dredging era of some ninety years past. A quick wander around failed to reveal any sheltered, out-of-the way tent sites. So, returning to the terminal we telephoned the B&B's in town – all five of them - but found them fully booked. Seems that the region was popular with bird watchers this time of year.

We had packed our baggage in four recycled cardboard boxes. This saved us from having to mail home a load of suitcases, which anyway we did not own. In these boxes was the bulk of our equipment, and food for the journey's initial few weeks. One of these boxes contained the tent and sleeping quilt – items needed the first evening. With permission from the friendly staff, we left the other three boxes in one corner of the terminal for the night, then stepped back outside just as they were locking up for the evening. Obviously, we would have to wait until morning to visit the freight terminal and collect our kayak.

The wind fairly bowled us half a mile east along the Snake River, and crossing a bridge we soon found a cranny semi-protected in the lee of a gravel bluff. This impromptu site was anything but secluded, being only 150 yards behind the Post Office annex. But it did feature a small stand of willow that would help shunt the wind, along with sparsely growing grass and moss that would serve as a measure of ground insulation. By ill design we had shipped our foam sleeping pads inside the kayak. Unlike a sleeping bag, our two-person quilt was simply an open blanket made with three-inch thick Primaloft synthetic insulation sandwiched between layers of nylon fabric. This arrangement saved weight and a great deal of precious cargo space inside the kayak. But this evening about all we had to place under us were our parkas and a few extra clothes. The permafrost was heat-sapping, and with no foam pads the night was actually the coldest of the entire trip.

Rain fell in the wee hours, and by morning the tent glistened in a sheen of ice.

Day 2: June 6 - Best laid plans

Breaking camp and returning to the air terminal, we collected the other three boxes and began lugging all four along the road leading around the airport. Air cargo was across the runway, but the road to it led the long way around. We had walked about a mile, stopping frequently to rest our arms, when a couple of friendly weather station employees stopped and offered us a lift.

Reaching the air cargo terminal we were pleased to find the kayak looking none the worse for its trip. We paid the freight, and left our boxes temporarily with the kayak.

The previous summer we had paddled the coast to Nome, then had continued another three hundred miles to the Inupiaq village of Shishmaref. That is where we wanted to begin this summer's trip. So our next order of business was to meet with a certain local pilot whom we had hired to fly the kayak to Shishmaref, strapped to the side of his Cub.

Rudy worked as a maintenance supervisor at one of the air terminals. He knew we were coming, so had borrowed a pick-up from one of his pilot friends, for use in collecting the kayak. He greeted us heartily and apologized for the truck, saying that the owner had laughed when he had asked to borrow it. Because of the remoteness and severe weather, vehicles here seemed to require a great deal of maintenance. At least this particular truck had four wheels and most of its engine presumably, and best of all it had a canoe rack.

The three of us piled into the cab, and Rudy cajoled the vehicle around the airport to the air cargo warehouses. Then with the kayak we returned to the main terminal. Mission Number One: a success.

Unloading the kayak beside Rudy's airplane, for the next hour we tried every possible way to fit the 20-foot boat to the 21½-foot airplane. Either the bow interfered with the propeller, or the stern with the horizontal control surface. We even tried fitting the kayak under the plane. But it was no go. The plane was too small for the job. Mission Number Two: a disappointing failure.

Several weeks ago we had phoned Rudy with the kayak's length, asking him to check it with a tape measure against his airplane. He had confirmed that the measurement checked out fine. So much for our carefully laid plans. But we had also been in touch with a Kotzebue pilot by the name of Buck Matson, who for a hefty sum could strap the kayak to his float plane there at his village, and fly it to Shishmaref. Now we tried telephoning Buck – repeatedly - but reached only his answering machine.

Far less appealing was a third option of loading the yak atop a taxi-van for Teller, which lies about part way between Nome and Shishmaref, and begin our journey from there. Thanking Rudy and leaving boat and boxes at the airport, we walked the few miles into town and talked with the Teller taxi driver. For an additional fee he agreed to transport the boat strapped to the roof of his van. But he also said that recent winds had driven the pack ice back into Port Clarence bay, and completely filled it. Now realizing that Teller's access to the sea was in question, we allowed the taxi to leave without us. This was just as well, since the kayak might have sustained a hammering on the rough two-hour drive.

With the passing of each hour we were growing more impatient to begin our journey. Perhaps overly eager, we decided to set off from here, and re-paddle the entire 300 miles to Shishmaref. This had taken us twelve days the previous summer, five of which had been stormbound.

By starting this summer's journey from Nome rather than Shishmaref, we would be putting ourselves at least a week behind schedule, and possibly two. The Arctic season is relatively short, so the delay would limit our chances of reaching our planned objective of Tuktoyuktuk, on Canada's north coast, before freeze-up at season's end. But at least we were familiar with the stretch from here to Shishmaref, and knew that it would make an ideal conditioner for our bodies and a shake-down for the kayak and gear. So with that decision made, we bought a gallon can of stove fuel - disallowed on the flight from home - and after a hearty lunch at Fat Freddy's restaurant we walked back to the airport, re-planning the days just ahead.

From the terminal we carried the yak a hundred yards across the road to the banks of the Snake River, and there removed its protective wrappings of cardboard and sheet plastic, which we then disposed of in the terminal's dumpster.

The bow had sustained some minor damage in transit, where something had struck it, and the port sheer was gouged in two places spaced about the same distance apart as the tines of a forklift – suggesting a careless driver. All these I repaired with dabs of epoxy, while Jenny returned to the terminal to fill our 2½ gallon water jugs. There she spoke with a couple of pilots who said that the ice had recently blown away from the coast at Shishmaref.

Changing into our expedition clothing, we packed our traveling clothes in a box, which Jenny then took to the Post Office annex and mailed home. Then we began loading the kayak for the short trip down the Snake River, to our previous night's campsite. The day had been windy and cold, with a bit of drizzle, but as we were packing, the sun managed to pierce the heavy clouds and a small but heartening patch of blue sky dispersed the encroaching gloom.

In the wake of last year's paddling adventures, this time we had come better prepared with heavier clothing and more of it, and a hefty load of food. Fortunately, it all fit in the boat's compartments, save for one bag, which we secured on deck with the bungees.

As we were readying for departure Rudy drove up and invited us to stay at his house for the night. Gratefully, we declined because we had already begun to condition ourselves to the cold, and knew that a sudden transition from indoors to out at sea could be severe.

Shoving off, we drifted in the crystal clear water while watching the bottom glide silently past. The Snake River is not large, perhaps 30 feet wide, nor does it actually "snake" in this vicinity; dredging had straightened it out, Paul Bunyan style. But it does connect with the sea, making an ideal waterway from the airport.

Reaching the bridge, we hauled out and carried everything in several loads to our previous campsite. I pitched the tent by simply re-attaching its lines to the same sticks pounded into the ground the previous evening and left as a contingency. Meanwhile Jenny walked back into town to buy fresh food from the grocery store.

Spartan camping behind the post office annex

Rain fell heavily in the "night," using the term loosely because the night did not get dark. As John Dyson quipped in his book *The Hot Arctic,* "You can tell the newcomers to the Arctic. They are the ones with flashlights in their kits."

Day 3: June 7 - Capsize!

Awaking at 5:30 am we found the morning very cold and sporadically rainy. Inside, the tent and its contents were soaked with condensation. A nearby airport windsock indicated brisk southwest winds, so we knew the seas would be fairly rough.

Breaking camp, we carried the kayak to the riverbank, both of us anxious in thought for the day's adventures. Then while I lugged bags of gear and food to the boat, Jenny packed them carefully into its three watertight compartments.

Despite the weather, the initial hour's paddling was quite pleasant. The river was calm and the current easy. For the few early risers driving to work, it was a headlights and windshield wipers type morning. Like most northern outposts, Nome seemed more like an indoor town this time of year. Not many people were seen braving the elements. The only other person outdoors this morning was a welder working on one of the barges.

The river emptied into the still waters of a small harbor turning basin. But when we reached the far end of this basin, the day's excitement began in earnest.

The outlet channel was narrow, and the river seemed eager to reach the sea. Suddenly the kayak was sucked into what resembled a giant washing machine, with tons of water undulating up and down the basin's ten-foot steel-slabbed concrete walls, and splashing mightily against them.

We had committed ourselves to the powerful outflow, and the closer to the sea, the larger and more bulbous were the waves rolling in. Rounding the final bend, we were greatly relieved to see that the entrance was not breaking. Still, the ride was wild, and we were glad to be wearing drysuits, warm hats beneath waterproof sou'westers, and neoprene paddling mitts.

The Chukchi Sea was choppy and far rougher than one would have expected in only 8 to 12 knots of wind. Obviously, the wind was blowing much stronger farther offshore. Accepting the wild ride and paddling with a will, we headed out into the gloom.

An immense man-made breakwater extends from the mainland. It blocked the way ahead and required us to paddle a stretch of open water to get around it. We then pointed the bow north along the fog-shrouded coast.

For the initial few miles the beaches were lined with tents and makeshift shelters cobbled together. Among them lay dredging equipment, buckets, gold pans, wooden crates and other prospecting paraphernalia. We did not envy the prospectors' work, but while taking the full brunt of the dreary elements we did notice their snug camps.

Hour after hour we continued ahead in the rain, with muscles beginning to complain of the prolonged and strenuous effort of bucking headwinds. Just as Dorothy had remarked to her little dog, "we're not in Kansas any more, Toto" we joked that we were not on Wickiup Reservoir any more either. The reservoir was near our home, and was where we had trained for several months, hoping in vain for big waves for practicing. Here on a normal day the waves were larger than they ever get on the reservoir.

Nevertheless, the spirit of adventure prevailed, and we were thrilled to have begun. Despite the inhospitable conditions we agreed that we would not have traded places with anyone.

Due to the recent change in plans, we lacked charts of this coast. The best we had found in Nome was a paper placemat from Fat Freddy's depicting the general area and drawn simply by hand. In retrospect this seems a bit foolhardy, but since we had traveled this same coast the previous summer we knew generally what to expect – at least over the long run. On a mile-by-mile basis, however, our memory method was proving less than effective because the fog prevented us from seeing any landmarks. The fog was so thick, in fact, that we had to keep as close to shore as we dared to prevent losing sight of it. In most places this was not very close, because the breaking surf extended a long ways out, and we certainly had to stay well outside that.

Rain fell heavily at times and the frigid air was laced with salt spray that splattered our eyeglasses. Time and again we wiped the lenses with the backs of our neoprene mitts, in order to maintain at least some visibility. Wiping our faces brought no relief because the mitts were ice-cold and soaking wet, and to the sensitive face they felt more like ice cubes.

By afternoon the waves had grown to five and six feet, and were now beginning to break over the yak and sometimes even us. Still, the kayak handled itself marvelously. It felt very stable and we were not worried about a capsize, despite the great distance to shore and the heavy surf pounding it.

After rounding a long, rocky coastline and negotiating a stretch of even more powerfully crashing waves, we came to a sandy beach and decided to attempt a landing. The surf was breaking a long ways out, and we knew that the ride to the beach would be wild. Exactly how wild we did not suspect.

The surf extended so far out that we could not time the wave sets over such a long distance. Catching a good lull, we raced it two-thirds the way in until overtaken by the next breaker. It shoved us heavily forward but we back-paddled out. Another wave followed, and we managed to back paddle out of it also. All seemed well until a much larger wave lifted the stern and shot us forward. The wave broke, dropped the yak down its seething face, and despite my ruddering hard to port and back-paddling fiercely, the kayak broached and capsized.

Head down in the smothering brine, I opened my eyes and was mildly surprised to see light. But that was all I could see – light. I could not see my spray skirt's release cord, nor could I find it by feel because my hands were cold and stiff, and were also encumbered in neoprene mitts. I let go of the paddle and thrashed out of the cockpit, relieved that the spray skirt popped off its rim as easily as it had during our training.

My head broke free of the water but I could see no sign of Jenny. So I made a few frantic swimming strokes to her cockpit and was just reaching under to drag her out - when she surfaced. Judging by her expression we seemed to be fine, so giving her a few encouraging words I ducked under the boat, came up on the other side, and swam to retrieve the paddles, which curiously were floating together.

Back at the upturned yak we sustained a few more breakers - with impunity for the most part - then decided to right the boat. This was easily done, except that the next onrush partially flooded the open cockpits. We could not turn the yak back over and land it upside down, because of the fragile cockpit comings and deck fittings. So we swam the boat toward shore until our feet found bottom, then began pushing and shoving, still taking a hammering from tempestuous waves.

On a past trip I had watched a partially flooded kayak break apart in surf, and was not about to let this happen to ours. We struggled mightily, trying to drag the boat from the water's tight grasp. The weight of water in the cockpits made this extremely difficult. But even more problematic, we seemed to have lost equilibrium. The stiffness borne of fatigue, the notorious shock of icy water against the eardrums, and the powerful back-wash were all causing us to stagger around as though punch drunk.

Before we could budge the stranded boat we needed to bail its cockpits, and before we could do that, we had to remove Jenny's life jacket and our two foam sleeping pads awash in her cockpit. These she had been using as cushioning and insulation. But then while we ambitiously bailed, I happened to notice the two pads had gone missing. The strong wind had taken them away. I dashed along the beach and found them tumbling in the surf. The initial night in Nome while sleeping on only a few clothes had taught us the value of these pads.

Safe ashore after the capsize

With the boat empty we easily carried it to higher ground. Thanks to our elastic-topped cockpit bags we had not lost any of our handy-type gear except for the hand towel that I had used that morning to mop the rain-soaked tent, and had simply tossed into the cockpit. Later I discovered that I had also lost my drysuit neck-ring, stowed loose in the cockpit also.

If nothing else, the mishap had reminded us to keep everything securely stowed. My point-and-shoot camera was, in fact, securely stowed - in the external pocket of my drysuit. Although advertised as "highly weather resistant," we knew all too well that a ten-minute swim in the Chukchi Sea exceeded the advertised claim. The camera had not survived, but at least we still had our SLR in its waterproof box.

The afternoon was wintry cold, and the wind was strong and laced with drizzle. Dragging the boat further up the beach to a flat, sandy area, we opened its three watertight compartments and found them indeed dry. From one of them we grabbed the tent then stumbled around looking for a level place to camp. And after pitching the tent we unloaded the boat's contents into it. The tent's interior was already sodden from the previous evening's condensation. And now most of our waterproof gear bags were soaked from the rain. Tossing in our sopping drysuits did not improve the domicile's ambience, but as we crawled inside we found it to be a huge improvement over the weather outside.

Seven and a half hours of paddling at an estimated speed of three knots, we estimated we had come about 22 nautical miles. Little did we realize how incorrect this figure was. We had not seen a single land feature all day, except for a large river emerging at the northwest end of a line of cabins. We lacked a proper chart on which to plot any GPS readings. And in our haste to depart, I had neglected to input Nome's coordinates into the GPS. The following morning the lifting fog revealed a steep slope immediately behind us. Examining a chart later, we saw that this slope is only 12 miles from Nome.

For an hour we mopped up, then crawled gratefully beneath the quilt. Warm and secure at last, we discussed the capsize. It had not been terribly frightening, nor life threatening thanks to our proximity to shore, to our waterproof drysuits, and our winter's emergency training on the reservoir.

During the broach and capsize, the kayak had lacked the maneuverability needed to turn out of the breaking wave, and it had seemed to trip over its sharply-veed bow. In jest, we called it the "Broach Coach." However, two months and 1,400 miles later, while paddling resolutely among the ice floes along the very top of Alaska, we more suitably christened her "Siku Kayak," which in the Inupiaq language means "sea-ice boat."

At this point in the journey the thought did not occur to us that we might have been better off not putting to sea in such inclement weather. The effort expended had hardly justified the scant mileage gained, nor the risks involved - especially along the rocky sections. Such was the price of our exuberance.

Along the way today we had paddled past areas where the gulls and terns were standing in shallow water, or hovering and diving as though fishing over shallow water. What was less obvious was that these were the river and creek outflows, otherwise obscured to us by the waves and fog. The birds were essentially showing us the location of fresh water flowing into the ocean. When in need of drinking water, these types of outflows would be important.

Day 4: June 8 - Strong headwinds

The wind remained strong during the night, but it did veer to north and reduce the seas by simply knocking them back. The surf was down to three feet, and was breaking only irregularly so that by timing our launch carefully we punched through without mishap. Departure time was 8:00 am, and compared with yesterday's conditions, the going was quite pleasant - at least by Arctic standards.

A seal surfaced nearby briefly, and even a bit of sunshine managed to shine through an otherwise ashen sky. The rain was holding off, and life was beginning to look up.

But after a couple of hours the headwinds strengthened, and reduced us to a mere crawl. At one point we labored past an iron sphere lying on the beach, which we recognized from the previous year. It looked like an explosive mine, but was probably an old buoy of some sort, about 3½ feet in diameter. Either way, we had a long look, since progress was so meager in the 20-knot headwinds. In the heavier gusts of perhaps twice that we actually found ourselves slipping backward despite our best efforts.

Another hour's struggle brought us to an area of driftwood in sufficient quantities to serve as protection from the wind. The type of tent we had brought required a wind block, we were finding. So we landed and seesawed the boat above high waterline – one of us lifting one end, shifting it a ways up the beach, setting it back down, then visa versa.

Typically, the first thing we did when landing, after scanning the surroundings for bears, was to examine the beach for their tracks. Not that we could do much about these huge beasts, but the more tracks, the more we tended to worry. Here the bear tracks were everywhere, but so were tracks of four-wheelers. Perhaps the locals were hunting the bears, or at least frightening them away and making them more leery of us humans.

Someone had built a couple of large hunting blinds or wind blocks from driftwood, so behind one of these we pitched the tent. This was not far from a nice spring seeping from the gravel. Again we were not certain of our position, but behind us we could see a group of low mountains, the northernmost in a line.

After securing camp and boat we went for a short walk onto the tundra. Here was the evidence of some sort of mining operation: a switchback cut on the hill above, and a number of old tent or cabin sites, long since overgrown in tundra. The tundra itself was lush and full of last year's berries, dehydrated now, and a few small flowers blooming cheerily

Visiting the region's only tree.

despite the day's unwelcoming chill. In such weather we could hardly imagine how the winter's snowpack had melted, and could only surmise that the previous weeks had been warmer. In the sand were tracks that looked like wolf and moose, and droppings that could have been caribou, or maybe only Arctic hare.

We walked along the beach a ways, curious about what had drifted in. This included a few whale and walrus bones, small muscle shells everywhere, a few birch bark rolls that we collected as emergency fire starters, and a few uncommonly large legs of Alaska King crabs.

Back at camp we hung our gear and clothing in the wind to dry, rinsed out salty mittens and hats, hastily sponged our bodies, then celebrated our presence in this interesting place with a hot cuppa each. We were reluctant to cook a meal because of the bears, so settled instead for a couple of cold sandwiches.

Jenny's wrist and forearm were swollen, fortunately not near any major tendons but painful nonetheless. We thought she might have bruised it during the capsize. Fortunately it did not bother her too much while paddling.

Day 5: June 9 - A hammering in the tent

After a refreshing sleep we rose early and found a fresh dusting of snow on the tent, the kayak, and in fact the entire landscape. The air was bracing, even though the wind had diminished to 10 to 15 northwest. We packed up and shoved off at 6:00 am, again timing the breakout very carefully to avoid mishap in the surf. Bucking headwinds again, the going was typically slow and strenuous. Still, we were not disappointed, but simply glad to be here and making the best of things while accepting the Arctic conditions for what they were - very boisterous at this time of year it seemed.

The rain was sometimes mixed with light grapnel. Again our drysuits were working very well, and the homemade neoprene booties were keeping our feet comfortably warm. We were not particularly cold while paddling except for our faces. Jenny's was periodically splashed by waves striking the bow, but mine was constantly splattered in the spray flung from her paddle blades. This is one disadvantage of a two-person kayak, and I can think of very few others.

Progress was sluggish, but we kept at it for 3 hours until coming to an area of wildly breaking seas extending several hundred yards offshore. The wind was blowing considerably harder out there, and I did not consider the situation entirely safe. So reluctantly we headed for shore, still at the early hour of 9:00 am. Just before touching land we underwent a few tense moments in the 3½-foot plunging shore break.

On shore we found one older set of bear tracks and a maze of fox and duck tracks. We searched several hundred yards in both directions, but could not find any natural or native-built windbreaks. Finally we settled on a spot at least somewhat protected behind a small bluff.

Increasing winds prompted us to relocate the tent into better protection, mainly by building a four-foot high windbreak of driftwood logs and sticks. Snow fell throughout the day, and even inside the tent we could see our breaths.

Jenny now realized how she had bruised her forearm. Actually it was not she, but me. As we were pitching the tent at the conclusion of Day 1, she was holding a driftwood stake when my driftwood mallet missed its mark and came down instead on her arm - fortunately well padded in clothing. Ever the stoic, she said it did not hurt much, so I assumed the blow had not connected with any force. Jenny is like that, not one to complain and always trying her best. A better companion this raddled adventurer could not have asked for.

Famished, we searched the area and found a cooking site a hundred yards from camp. Crouching in the lee of a bluff we cooked a pot of corn spaghetti - our first hot meal of the trip.

Back in the tent we listened to it flog in the powerful and gusty wind. We felt extremely apprehensive about it collapsing. Clearly, we needed a stronger tent. A tent failing within a day's walk of one's car would be trouble enough, but out here on the remote Arctic coastline it could be life threatening.

The previous summer we had been stormbound five days on a beach between York Cliffs and Wales - quite a few miles ahead. That stretch of coast lacked sufficient driftwood for building a windbreak, and the thought of being stranded there during a major storm, with this feeble tent blown to tatters, was unthinkable. The feelings of vulnerability imparted by this tent were growing so strong that we decided that if the wind were still blowing west in the morning, for our own safety we would return to Nome and see about acquiring a stronger tent.

Day 6: June 10 – Turnaround

Rising early, indeed we found the wind still blowing west - though not as strong at this early hour. Breaking through the surf at 8:15 am, we pointed the bow back toward Nome.

For the first time we were paddling this particular boat in strong following seas. So the motions felt strange and took some getting used to. A breaking sea overtook us, and for a few long moments we struggled to free the yak from another broach. Perhaps we were merely over-reacting, and that any kayak would have undergone the same difficulties, we reasoned. But from a design standpoint I planned my next boat for a more rounded fairbody forward, which would allow it to slide laterally, and more vee aft to reduce weather-vaning. I also found that downwind paddling required a lot more rudder control, probably for the same reasons.

Even paddling vigorously, we were surprised to take 1½ hours to reach our previous campsite over a distance that had taken twice that going into the wind. At times the down-winding was a real challenge, mainly because the wind was blowing 20 and gusting even harder. Occasionally we rested, and even then the shore slid briskly by, such was the driving force of the wind at our backs. The sun was shining weakly through thin, high clouds, but its glare was reflecting powerfully off the water directly ahead. This reduced visibility and required a great deal more caution. Gusts were tearing sand from the beaches in great billows and flinging them into the air, and the sun's backlighting was emphasizing and making them all the more dramatic. We saw one seal, and several types of small land and sea birds including ducks and terns.

Rounding the jetty in boisterous conditions, we paddled toward the Snake River entrance and landed on the beach just east of it. This was the same place where we had landed the previous year on our way north. The return trip had taken 5½ hours, compared with 13½ outbound. This suggested that we had actually done quite well in the adverse headwinds.

Leaving me watching the gear, Jenny hastened to a telephone and phoned the accommodations in town, finding but a single night's vacancy. When she returned to the beach with a cab, the driver took one look at the kayak and offered to radio for a Suburban.

Jenny rode with the first driver while I stood on the Suburban's rear bumper, hanging onto the kayak and chatting with a friend of the driver's helping me do the same. Rolling slowly along main street, we took the brunt of a few gawking tourists. By happenstance we were following a police car going slowly also. The other fellow joked that we were in a parade. I bantered that we *were* the parade.

Checking into the Bed and Breakfast we took full advantage of its hot showers and laundry. Somewhat re-civilized, and sufficiently so for the likes of Nome, we walked into town for a hearty meal at Fat Freddy's.

Back at the B&B we enjoyed visiting with the owners Larry and Corinne, who like most Nome residents were as congenial as they were interesting. Larry worked as a pilot for one of the airlines, and Corinne an administrator for a competing airline. Recently they had remodeled their home and accommodations, first traveling to Seattle to purchase the necessary tools and materials, and then having them air freighted to Nome. For sport they both jumped out of perfectly good airplanes while wearing parachutes. They showed us a video of themselves in free-fall, and dragged out their skydiving gear. It looked like great fun to us.

Retiring to our room to evade a pair of house cats wreaking havoc with my allergies, we made dozens of phone calls in an attempt to order a new tent, to reach Buck Matson, and to find other options for the kayak's transport to Shishmaref.

Day 7: June 11 – success

With great relief we were able to order a new tent. Never mind its seven large-diameter poles and whopping eleven pounds of weight; the salesman claimed it was strong enough to support a person sitting on top of it. So we figured it should handle the Arctic storms pretty well.

In addition, we ordered a waterproof camera to replace the "water resistant" one that had drowned in the beach swim.

The new tent was on its way to Shishmaref, but the kayak was not, so the trip still seemed a little dubious. The kayak was too large to fit in any of the local commuter planes. But in addition to good ol' Buck with his floatplane in Kotzebue, we now had two more leads. One was to strap it to a Cessna 185 owned by one of the local airlines, and the other was to load it into a much larger DC3.

Buck finally answered his phone, and yes, he could fly the yak from Kotzebue to Shishmaref. Kotzebue has a large airport and we could easily ship the kayak from here to there. But to avoid that extra step, and Buck's relatively large fee, we concentrated instead on the 185.

The pilot submitted a request with the FAA for an external load permit, and was told to contact Buck Matson for details. We had little confidence in that arrangement, knowing that Buck did not answer his phone any old time it rang. The 185 pilot finally called to say he could not manage it. Instead he recommended the DC-3, saying it would soon be flying for Shishmaref on a scheduled run north. This sounded good, until we asked about the price - $2,500. We were not sure what monetary frame of reference this fellow was using, but it certainly differed from ours. So much for those options, now we needed to get back in touch with Buck.

The B&B had been previously booked, so we landed back on the streets, grateful that at least Larry and Corinne extended us the use of their garage for storing our gear, and their front porch for the kayak.

Wandering through town we happened to meet a clerk at a gift shop. Mary Haydon kindly agreed to handle any messages on our behalf. So from a pay phone we left a message with Buck saying that we were air freighting the kayak to Kotzebue, and did we need to be in Kotzebue ourselves to help load it onto his float plane? The next morning Buck called Mary, saying that we did not need to be in Kotzebue, but that he would fly the kayak to Shishmaref as soon as he heard we were there. Now we were getting somewhere.

In the back of another old Suburban we hauled the kayak to the airport. The cargo company did not offer direct flights to Kotzebue, so the yak would first return to Anchorage, where it would then be loaded onto a plane for Kotzebue. Even so, the total cost was a very reasonable $44.

Leaving the kayak at the terminal, we returned to our original campsite behind the Postal Annex.

Days 8,9: June 12-13 - Preparations

The next morning we shifted to a nicer camping place on top of the hill, one that afforded more seclusion as well as a commanding view of the sprawling, if somewhat ramshackle community.

The day was windy but sunny. Not warm enough to wander around without parkas, but very pleasant nonetheless. For half a day the wind blew southeast, then reverted back to its prevailing west and northwest.

To show Mary appreciation for her message taking, we invited her to dinner. She, in turn, invited us to visit her home – or at least the place where she was house sitting. As a bonus we were able to get showers.

Walking along the dusty streets of Nome, we happened to see a load of kayaks on a van. Following it, we met Keith Conger, just returning from a week-long youth excursion. He invited us to his house to see his favorite kayaking gear – gear that was suitable for these northern climes. His native wife Annie happened to be related to our friends the Nayokpuks in Shishmaref. The Congers invited us to a barbecue, but we had already gorged ourselves at Fat Freddy's.

We booked a flight to Shishmaref for the following morning, and checked our baggage. There we met Stacy Loucks, a good friend from the previous summer. She told us about her travels to Egypt, where she had worked with an archeological expedition. At one point she had stopped the caravan and climbed over a hill for a pit stop, and discovered a lost mine. It turned out to be an archeologist's bonanza, and they named the site for her.

Corinne worked in an office upstairs, and said that the previous evening she had driven around for an hour looking for us. Skydiving friends of theirs had arrived in town, and were looking for potential customers interested in tandem dives. We were sorry to have missed the fun.

Day 10: June 14 – Shishmaref at last

Rising early, we broke camp and walked in a drizzle to the air terminal. A reporter for the Nome Nugget introduced himself, and we figured that Mary must have contacted him. He interviewed us about our journeys past and present, and took a few photos. We told him that Nome was one of the highlights of our trip, thanks to the friendly people – people like Larry and Corinne, Mary, Stacy and her sister Nikki, and dozens of others who had been very friendly to us.

Still, we were glad to be moving on, and could only hope that the yak would find its way to Shishmaref. Buck had been so difficult to contact that we were not altogether certain this plan would work. But we seemed to have run out of alternatives.

The plane took off in a pummeling rain, and during most of the flight the visibility was nil. Not until descending below 2,000 feet over Shishmaref did we finally break out of the clouds. Landing uneventfully, the plane taxied to the terminal, and after the pilot had shut down the engines he turned around and asked how we were going to get our kayak to here. He seemed to know a lot about our trip, such is life in these far-flung parts.

Curtis and Sheryl Nayokpuk, good friends from last year, now worked for this airline and were here to greet its passengers, and to deliver its freight. Right away they recognized us, and were as friendly as ever. They were going to Nome for the day, and welcomed us to stay in their home. We thanked them, but said we were quite comfortable sleeping outside, and that we wanted to make camp at our old familiar site. We were halfway there lugging our gear when Curtis came by with his 4-wheeler, and kindly transported our bags to the shoreside east of the runway, where we had camped at the conclusion of our journey the previous summer.

I pitched the old tent and secured our gear inside. Jenny rode with Curtis back to the terminal, and from there another Nayokpuk – Russel - drove Jenny and a load of boxed goods to the Nayokpuk General Store, in town. There she helped unload the cargo, then telephoned Buck and left word of our arrival.

Jenny returned, then we both tramped back to the General Store and talked with yet more Nayokpuks, Walter and Percy - both as personable as always. The previous summer Percy had taught us the Inupiaq pronunciation of the word "kayak." The Inupiaq language is harshly guttural, and consonants are pronounced forcefully. Their speech can be heard above all others in a noisy crowd, and I would not be surprised if the language was specialized for utility in stormy weather and high winds. The pronunciation of "kayak" has no English counterpart, but would be like clearing the back of one's throat forcefully to pronounce the first part of the word, then suddenly stopping with another hard and gutteral "K."

Next we visited with Albert Ningeulook at his home, and chatted amicably with him awhile. Albert had a penchant for meeting famous people, and his walls and bookshelves displayed photos of famous personalities and books autographed to him personally. He showed us a letter from Bill Clinton, saying that the president had even telephoned him to make sure he had received it. The president told Albert it was the first time in years that he had sat down at his typewriter to write a personal letter. This was in response to a poem that Albert had written and sent to the White House, in condolences for the families of the fatalities in the Brown airplane crash.

Albert's brother was also visiting, and told us about a book he was writing on the history of the region. Both of these native fellows were extremely well educated and interesting to talk with.

Proceeding to the post office, we were thrust back to square one when we learned that our new tent had not arrived.

Back at camp I heard a distant airplane. As it drew slowly closer I saw that it was a floatplane carrying a kevlar-colored kayak! Grabbing our aircraft VHF, I radioed Buck but received no reply. The plane circled and landed in the expansive lagoon adjacent the northeast end of town. This was three quarters of a mile from our camp. Jenny was just returning from her third trip into town, so together we ran along the lagoon's shore and greeted Buck as he was wading the kayak through the expansive shallows toward shore.

This was indeed a momentous occasion, with kayakers and kayak finally reunited in Shishmaref, and ready to begin the trip in earnest. Or nearly so, for we were still waiting for the new tent.

Buck was very personable, and apologized for his reticence. Of course we understood that like many long-time Alaskans he was not overly fond of telephones – or aircraft radios either for that matter. He had not even checked his messages today, but said he figured we must be here by now, since he knew the weather was adequate. It was barely adequate, as far as I could tell, and we had not been expecting him on a day like this, with low clouds and drizzle.

Buck complemented the kayak, saying it was "a dream to fly" compared with the canoes he normally transported. This was due to its better streamlining and enclosed deck. I asked about the ice in Kotzebue Sound, and Buck said it was sporadic, concentrated at Cape Espenberg, and extending about a third of the way across the sound. Percy had said that the pack ice was 30 miles west of Shishmaref, and cautioned us that a strong west wind could bring it back.

A local fellow, Cliff Weiyouanna, drove his truck out into the shallow water, and the four of us talked for a while, with Cliff seated in his truck, Buck standing in hip waders, and Jenny and me barefoot in five inches of very cold Arctic Lagoon. Soon Jenny and I were standing in the kayak instead, bracing against the truck.

Cliff proved to be a fascinating fellow himself. He owned the yellow Cub we had seen parked at the airport, and a herd of about a thousand reindeer. Asked how he came to own them, he replied: "I bought them." Each year he hired a helicopter to herd the animals into corrals for de-horning, and for butchering a few for their meat and skins. The horns he boxed and sent to a Korean firm. "I don't care what they do with them," he said, "as long as they pay me for them." He said he had been busy the past few weeks laying up his supply of oogruk, or bearded seal meat.

Jenny and I carried the kayak back to camp, elated to have it here. It had come through in fine shape save for one contusion to the deck just aft the center hatch.

Days 11-14: June 15, 16, 17, 18 – Waiting for the tent

The area of our campsite was most interesting, and in the next five days of waiting for the new tent we came to know this area well. The village stood half a mile away, improbably perched on a long but narrow island that more resembled an overgrown sand bar. The site had been chosen long ago for its access to the Chukchi Sea, renowned in former times for its bountiful fishing, sealing, and whaling. Separating the island from the mainland is the Arctic Lagoon. Looking southwestward across the widest part, called Shishmaref Inlet, land may or may not be visible, depending on the atmosphere's clarity. It is 16 miles away. The place we camped this year was the same place as the previous year, but a little off to one side because ATV tracks had since damaged the vegetation. Now we were only 30 feet from the edge of the lagoon and hardly three feet above it. Its waters slopped melodically onto the shoreline.

The ground was vibrant with tundra – mostly grasses gaily embellished with ground hugging willow, Labrador tea, and a scattering of colorful wildflowers: northern primrose, coltsfoot, roseroot, and the inevitable dandelion. Many of last year's blueberries still clung to their stout stems, and even though now dehydrated, we had seen one family collecting them.

Albert said this area had a long history as a gathering and camping place for itinerant hunting and fishing parties. They dug pits in the sand dunes and lined them with driftwood, for use as food storage cellars. A few of these pits were still in evidence, and one appeared not to have been opened in a long while.

Hidden in the grasses were a few old rusty fisherman-type anchors and an old bronze port, or window, that had probably come from a wrecked whaling ship. Someone must have found it elsewhere and brought it to here.

Near our camp was an ancient umiak frame, it's wooden frames sagging. The umiak was the multiple passenger version of the kayak, used mainly for whaling. The age of this frame would have been anyone's guess. Such items do not rot in the Arctic, for rotting requires bacteria, and this does not flourish in the extreme climate. Instead, things simply wither.

This is also why the Arctic produces so much peat, because of the vegetation's slow rate of decay.

Among the assorted junk were a few massive but discarded outboard engines. Despite their enormous cost, the service life of one of these beasts is usually just a few years. This is because they lead hard lives. Most are operated throttles wide open, propelling the large home-built plywood skiffs as fast as they would go. And understandably so, for the distances are vast and the periods of suitable weather brief. The sea is open only a few short months each year, and for most of the remaining time these engines lay buried beneath snow and ice. It was during this time that the electrolytic effects of the salt water perhaps took their greatest toll.

Things are not thrown away in these northern villages, since they might be found useful later on. Nearby was a dismantled wall tent that appeared to be still useable. We had seen this heap of faded white canvas and metal poles last summer, in exactly the same spot. It had not been touched except by the winter storms.

Most useful to us were a few sheets of plywood and poles of driftwood found lying about. The next approaching gale had us running around gathering these items with which to construct a wind-block for our sadly inadequate tent.

This tent had a single curved pole at each end, bringing to mind the Conestoga wagon of the mid 1700's. It was to be staked at each end, then tensioned mightily to reduce flogging. Eighty pounds of tension was sometimes needed, according to the manufacturer. This outrageous requirement called for extremely stout stakes. We used poles of driftwood pounded into the ground until they struck permafrost. But even thus tensioned, the tent flapped and rattled with a vengeance. The manufacturer claimed that a windbreak causes turbulence, which, in turn makes the tent flap. But we tried pitching it in the open, only to watch it strain nearly to the break point. Clearly, this tent needed constant protection from the wind, which here at Shishmaref was my plywood enclosure. This enclosure was open to the sides, so it required me to shift it around with each shift in wind direction.

As the days wore on, the weather became much more pleasant, with temperatures soaring into the high 50's by day, and dipping merely to the high 30's by night. Gone were the nights when we slept beneath the quilt in all our clothing, including parkas. Now we were down to quilt and long underwear. The short Arctic summer was upon us, and we were still waiting for the tent, trying to resist the favorable paddling weather urging us on.

In the absence of the icy, frigid wind, the mosquitoes made their summer's debut – not in clouds here on this wind-blessed island, which no doubt was another reason for its selection as a village site, but just a few buzzing about. As an alternative to applying commercial repellant, we began taking a daily dose of B-vitamins and brewer's yeast. So far this seemed to be working.

Lemmings scurried this way and that, through tunnels and along well-worn trails connecting their many burrows. These overgrown, short-tailed mice were staple for fox and jaeger, so tended to keep their aboveground appearances brief. Occasionally one would pause and stare at us for a few long moments. They were feeding on the new and ample grasses and willow shoots, and never disturbed our food or gear.

The local ambiance was also blessed with a few moose heads lying about. At first we thought they were discarded, but Albert told us that, no, they were curing. Decayed - again as opposed to rotted - moose brains were considered a delicacy here, he explained. We were not tempted to try them.

During the first few days we had noticed a kittiwake on the beach nearby, and finally realized it was living there. On somewhat closer inspection we saw that one of its wings was broken. It appeared quite healthy otherwise, and before long we became friends. It allowed us to approach nearly to within touching distance, and accepted our morsels of food. Once it held out its wing as if to show us what had happened. A bullet perhaps had shattered the outer joint. We named the poor creature Dilbert, and enjoyed watching it forage along shore, or swim in the waters looking for tidbits. We even discussed adopting Dilbert as our mascot, and taking him with us - mainly for his own safety. We suspected he had adopted us as protection from the fox, which dwell all along these coasts.

On the morning of the 18th I went to visit Dilbert, and found him dead. Some of his feathers lay strewn around his lifeless body, and imprinting the sand nearby were tracks of hip waders. I turned him over, and found the fatal wound. To the person who had shot him, Dilbert was just another bothersome seagull. To us he was an important link in the web of life, a creature of nature with a will and a right to the gift of life. He had shown a genuine personality and accepted us with no apparent resentment for the human who had shot him the first time. Turning sadly back to camp, I tossed the two cookies I had saved for our friend into the sea.

The following evening two teenagers tramped past wearing hip waders and carrying a .22 rifle. The people here lived by different rules, ones tempered by survival in this harsh and unforgiving land. What may have seemed callous to us was perhaps necessary for their existence. Seagulls were notorious for pecking and contaminating the fillets of fish hanging to dry, and tearing up the animal hides. So they had to be dealt with accordingly.

Day after day we waited for the new tent. Every time we decided to press on without it, another williwaw threatened to flatten this flimsy tent, shaking not only it, but also some sense back into us.

Each time a plane landed we scurried to the terminal to watch it unload – but to no avail. Jenny placed several phone calls to the post offices in Nome and Anchorage, trying to track our parcel. Someone suggested we phone the various taxi planes in Nome, and ask them to check the cargo in their warehouses. They said that cargo was often stockpiled until constituting a full load. Yet the postmaster here claimed that this was not the case with the mail, that the air taxis were required to carry all mail to the villages right away.

During one of her daily trips to the terminal to check for our parcel, Jenny noticed a kabloona (white stranger) stepping off the plane. The woman climbed onto the back seat of Shishmaref's open-air taxi truck. The taxi driver, Sheryl Nayokpuk's, Curtis' wife, offered Jenny a lift into town. The woman boasted of working for the Department of Labor, but otherwise had very little to say, despite Jenny's attempts at conversation. Jenny later told me the woman was shivering like a fish out of water. This served to remind us how we were starting to adapt to these northern climes. We were becoming more like the hardy locals.

The Inupiaq continued to show their friendliness and hospitality. Everyone knew that "the kayakers" were still here. The storekeepers welcomed us, the women outside their houses waved hellos to us, the kids riding by on their 4-wheelers smiled and waved timidly. The place was starting to feel like home. Cliff Weyouianna repeatedly invited us to stay in his house, saying that he had two empty bedrooms upstairs. He also welcomed us to stop by for a meal anytime. "Just don't mind the mess," he quipped.

In many Inupiaq villages, seals are fed to the dogs.

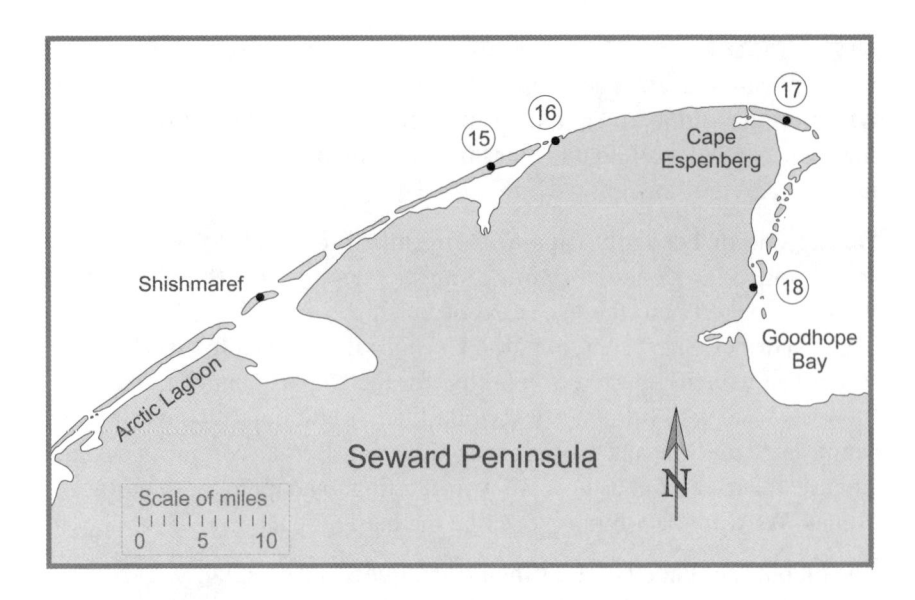

One afternoon a large hovercraft ran onto the beach with engine trouble. Locals flocked around, including us, and I was able to talk with the captain and learn about these outrageously noisy but still very interesting monsters.

And speaking of engine trouble, later in the day a four-engine cargo plane landed with the same type of problem. The pilots could not restart number two. Hours later a second cargo plane landed, presumably with parts. The plane with the stricken engine finally took off with only three engines running, without difficulties. For such a small and remote village, Shishmaref seemed to be enjoying its share of excitement.

Day 15: June 19 - Departure

A gentle but steady rain had been soaking the landscape all day, but by evening was letting up. Enough waiting was enough. New tent or no, we were going.

We broke camp and packed our things, then carried the yak to water's edge and loaded it there. The time was 9:00 pm, and the only one to see us depart was a friendly sled dog puppy that had recently been hanging about camp.

The Hovercraft happened to be leaving as well, and again several locals turned out to watch it. But one couple drove down to the shore specifically to wave to us, and from a distance we thought they looked like Curtis and Sheryl.

Paddling the length of the island, we dragged the yak over a shallow bar, then found a strong out-flowing current that whisked us to sea. For a while we enjoyed tailwinds, but these dwindled and swung round to various points of the compass. The sky ahead looked horrific, almost as though a hurricane was brewing. Oddly this belied the near calm conditions now on the surrounding sea. The moiling blackness was only a cloud dump ahead of us, and moving away.

Our first patch of shore-bound ice was stranded on shore and not touching the water. About the size of a school bus, it was a spectacular blue color, but also quite dirty on the surface. Farther along was a larger patch, visible for several miles and gleaming through the gloom like a beacon. Away from the lagoon inlets, the water was crystal clear, and even in fifteen feet of water we could see clam and muscle shells lying on the seabed.

We also saw many types of birds, one porpoise, and a few seals foraging at the lagoon entrances. In 5 hours and 20 minutes we covered 17.4 NM straight line from Shishmaref on the GPS. But the five-plus hours of unaccustomed sitting in the kayak had our lower bodies feeling numb. So for improved circulation I decided to walk along the sandy beach while pulling the kayak behind me. This worked marvelously. The tramping was easy, my lower body circulation was restored, and very little pull was required to tow the boat. Jenny said she felt like Robert Service's "bloated plutocrat." My turn came, and I, too, found that being towed was great fun. It was rather like being on holiday.

While Jenny was lining, she saw in the distance what looked like a dead baby seal on the beach. Not dead, just napping. It was mottled grey and furry, with big eyes that immediately melted a person's heart. I landed and took a few pictures, never mind that the day was rather too dark for photographs because of the heavy cloud cover – a problem that would plague our photographs for the journey's duration. The little fellow was not in the least timid, but when we approached within a few feet, it spread it claws and growled. We backed off, and right away it relaxed. As we were leaving, it had gone back to sleep.

Later we found another of these interesting creatures, and again stopped for pictures. Obviously no grizzly bears were present around here, for these little seals would have been like sitting ducks. Unfortunately, ATV tracks were present. On Shishmaref we had seen three or four hundred dogs, most used for sled dog racing at the expense of the local seal and fish populations. Differing cultural and economic viewpoints once again.

Eight miles of lining the kayak reinforced our satisfaction with our homemade neoprene booties. They were easy to walk in, and being waterproof they allowed us to step into puddles with impunity.

While lining the beach we were seeing strange drag marks, and finally realized they were from the Hovercraft. The vehicle was headed for Kotzebue at 30+ knots, and was apparently following the coast so closely that at times it ran onto the beaches, obviously with no ill effects.

While paddling in the wee hours past midnight we watched with curiosity a simultaneous sunset and sunrise. The sun was barely dipping below the horizon, such that to its left was a sunset, while to the right was a sunrise. This phenomenon was the result of our proximity to the Arctic Circle at nearly Summer Solstice.

After paddling all night and covering 30½ miles, we stopped at 7:00 am - now June 20 - and pitched the tent among the dunes. Nearby was a large dome of sand, and behind that, a reindeer corral. The air was chilly and thick with the morning dew, and the ground wet from recent rain. The air was still, so the old tent sufficed. In it we slept five hours.

Day's Run: 30½ nautical miles, 10 hours. Camp: 66° 29.43' N, 165° 01.58' W

Day 16: June 20 - continued

Jenny cooked a pot of chorizo: half a pound of ground beef, four eggs, and a packet of seasoning mix. We set off at 3:00 pm with a 10-knot north wind in choppy seas that of course increased the efforts. We paddled past a couple more beach-lounging seal pups, and in one area came to the abominable sight of four walrus carcasses minus heads. These animals were enormous. The first one was half submerged, and from a distance we thought it might have been a polar bear. Nevertheless, we were most discouraged to see these hapless animals slaughtered for their ivory tusks.

A walrus

For two and a half hours we battled the headwinds, or at least winds fine on the port bow, but finally decided to call a halt. After the all-night stint at the paddles, we were ready for more sleep. Landing ashore at 5:30 pm, we made camp among the dunes.

Behind this camp was an expanse of tundra pockmarked with ponds of all descriptions, and beyond those the Arctic Lagoon stood less than a quarter mile away. Its water looked flat, but we could also see that the lagoon terminated a mile or two to the northeast, meaning that it would not serve as an easier avenue for our travels. In the distance to the right stood a solitary cabin. We had seen enough of these to know that it probably belonged to a native family and was used either for summertime fishing and hunting, or for wintertime trapping and hunting. Far across the lagoon, the bank gleamed with a long line of snow.

Time and again we reflected on our enjoyment of this trip. Exploring the wild and pristine coast was a genuine pleasure and privilege. The harsh weather keeps most people at bay, and this was good because most did not respect the land enough to stop impacting it with litter and so-called development. We had acclimatized to both the weather and the immensity of the landscape itself, and thanks largely to the two years of making our way slowly and laboriously north, we felt like we had earned the right to be here, or nearly enough so. A few hundred years ago we would have encountered many Inupiat, and a few hundred years into the future and we might possibly encounter many once again. But for now we were in an interim where the people were few and their impact quite small. This was just how we liked it.

Day's Run: 6½ mi. in 2½ hrs. Camp: 66° 31.868' N, 164° 46.461' W

Day 17: June 21 – Summer Solstice

Ready for departure, we positioned the kayak at water's edge with its bow pointing to sea. Jenny sat in her cockpit with her spray-skirt attached. Not wearing my spray skirt, I fitted it to my cockpit coaming and drew the waste opening tight. Timing our breakout carefully, I shoved the boat out then climbed aboard and rode it through the surf seated on the afterdeck. Once past the breakers, I opened my spray skirt's waist opening and slid down into my seat. That done, at 10:30 am we were off into a boisterous sea.

Glorious sunshine was glaring from directly ahead, and for the occasion Jenny was already wearing her sunhat. I had unwisely stowed mine in the aft compartment. The glare quickly reminded me that yesterday I had fried my eyes by not wearing my dark glasses. So kneeling in my cockpit, I turned around and opened the hatch to retrieve my hat - such was the kayak's great stability.

The headwinds were fine on the port bow to 10 knots. Otherwise the day was gorgeous with plenty of blue sky. As the day wore on, the winds diminished, and the day became one of the more beautiful Arctic interludes imaginable. We felt almost as though in Mexico's Sea of Cortez. However, a dip of the hand into the Chukchi Sea put us back at the proper latitude. That latitude was 66° 33', the Arctic Circle. And we happened to be crossing it on June 21, the day of Summer Solstice!

More headless walrus littered the beaches, six or eight plus a few smaller carcasses. A short while later, a porpoise swam in our vicinity for a few minutes. Then to our joy we paddled past three more infant seals snoozing on the beaches. Once past the final lagoon entrance, which was enormous, the coast became more rugged with irregular sand bluffs, steep cutbanks, and also quite a bit of snow.

Jenny had been using her neck ring all day and once again finding it to her liking. The drysuits featured rubber neck-gaskets to seal out the water. Our homemade rings expanded this rubber away from the skin for some much-needed ventilation. Unfortunately, I had lost mine in the capsize. But the afternoon warmed considerably and we paddled with drysuits zipped open.

For much of the day the surf had prevented an easy landing. But by afternoon it diminished, and finally allowed Jenny to step ashore. She lined the yak for half an hour until we reached the riverside settlement of Espenberg. No habitation was in evidence among the solitary three or four houses.

We paddled for another few miles and began talking about a direct crossing of Kotzebue Sound. The sea was invitingly calm, and we could see mountains on the far side. At its narrow mouth, the Sound is about 30 miles wide. A direct crossing would save us hundreds of miles of paddling the long way around, and at least a week or possibly two.

A few animals were wandering about shore, but we could not decide exactly what they were. At first I thought they might be moose, but as we drew closer we could see that each had only two legs. So we thought they might be people. A lack of trees or other identifiable objects for size reference makes it very difficult to judge the size of anything. My two moose turned out to be four sandhill cranes. This brought to mind a similarly humorous incident the previous year, when we had mistaken cranes for grizzly bears. For the same reasons we also found it difficult to judge the size of the surf when viewed from out at sea. The day of the capsize we had grossly underestimated that.

We landed safely ashore for a cuppa. In the absence of wind the mosquitoes swarmed about, so Jenny smeared on a few dabs of repellent. The bugs were not bothering me, thanks to my greater intake of B vitamins and brewer's yeast. A few bugs bit me, but this only suggested my intake had not been quite sufficient. Still, in view of the buzzing hordes, this experiment was working surprisingly well.

A few miles farther we decided that if we were to jump the 30-mile gap to Talikoot on Cape Krusenstern, this would be the place. The weather was so perfect that it tempted us to set off right away. But since we had already come 27 miles today, prudence suggested that we first rest. So at 8 pm we landed and pitched the tent in the dunes near a small river.

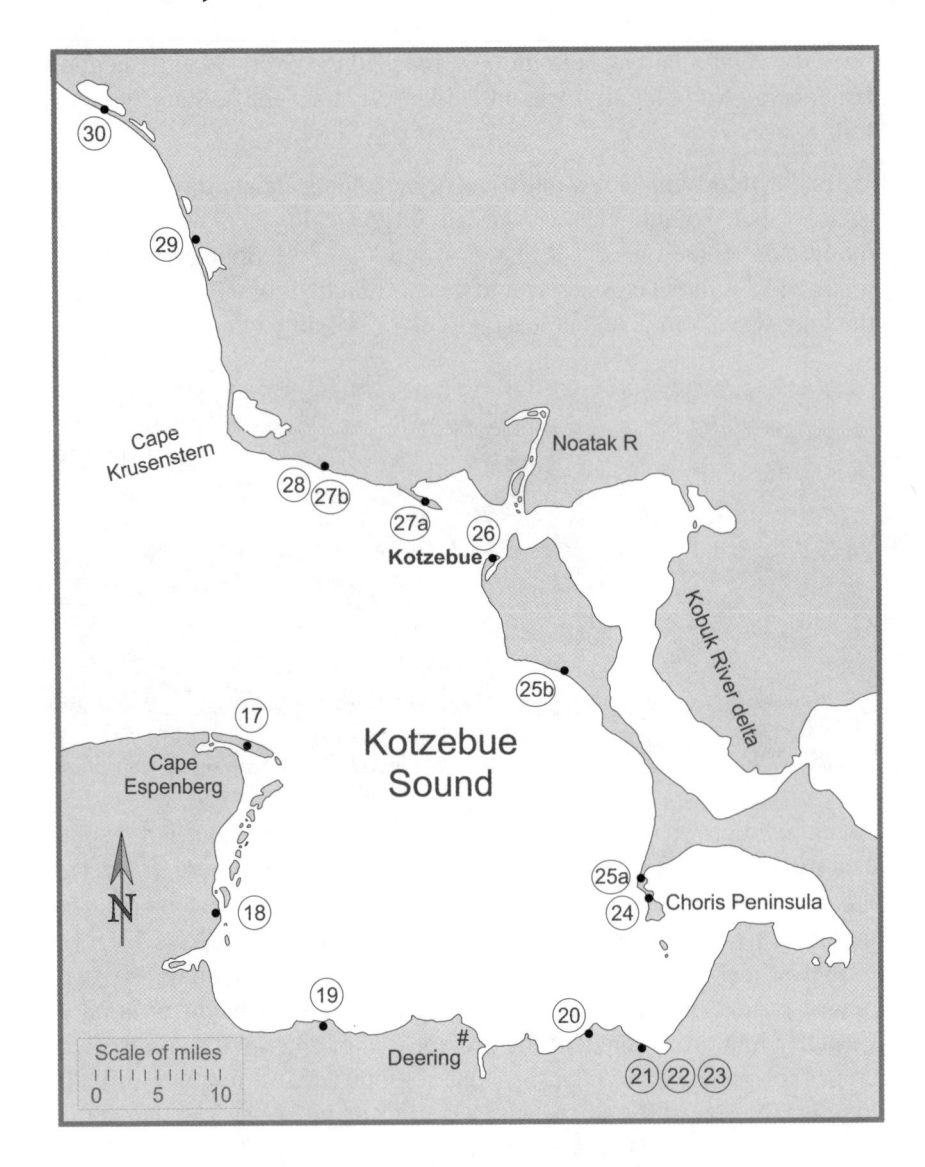

I crawled into the tent to escape the bugs, but the sun was glaring and the tent's interior soon grew untenably warm, even with one sidewall unzipped wide open. So I joined Jenny at the creek for a most refreshing bath, minus soap. The water was not icy cold by any means, thanks to the effects of solar warming. One advantage of the B-vitamin method was that I did not contaminate the water with chemical repellent. Neither had I contaminated my skin, which absorbs much of the repellent. But for some reason, after the bath the mosquitos started landing on me more.

Day's Run: 27 n-mi, 9½ hrs. Camp: 66° 35.394' N, 163° 47.296' W

Day 18: June 22 – Around the Sound

The decision not to cross the sound was made for us the next morning. We awoke early to find the wind blowing a hefty 10-15 west. This came as a disappointment, but it also brought relief because we knew that paddling across could have been very risky, due to the possibility of a sudden storm. And indeed, such a storm was soon to come steamrolling in.

With the pressure off, I left Jenny sleeping, and wandered across the expansive tundra a ways into the interior for a look around. The soft green carpet I walked upon stretched away to distant green-grey hills. The tundra itself was not totally flat, but rose upon low mounds and dipped into seasonal drainages, and was punctuated by small ponds. The nearest pond was occupied by several ducks and a few cranes, along with one very large, white swan. Strewn across the ground were small wildflowers with a few scraggly clumps of stunted willow three or four inches high at most.

I remembered reading a few interesting books by a certain author about exotic places he had visited. I enjoyed them, until in one place he described a very brief trip to the Arctic tundra. There, he told of walking away from camp and experiencing extreme revulsion for the utter vastness and so-called "emptiness." At that point I realized this fellow was merely a tourist. How different were my own views of the Arctic tundra. To me it is exquisitely beautiful, peaceful and serene, like nature had finished creating it only weeks earlier, yet home to subsistence cultures since the Ice Ages and possibly eons earlier. If the Arctic had no redeeming qualities, why then did birds migrate to here each summer in their millions, along with whales and caribou? In summer this is their home, and in my estimation is one of the most beautiful homes imaginable. To me, the vastness is elbow room, a quality so lacking in the civilized world. This quality has always attracted explorers and adventurers. I found it invigorating to the soul.

We set off at 11:00 am beneath a sky mostly clear, save for a smudge of cirrus on the western horizon. The wind was on our starboard quarter, giving us a nice boost the remaining seven miles to the tip of Cape Espenberg.

Quickly the cirrus moved across the entire sky while shoving a small band of cumulus ahead of it. When we reached a light beacon denoting the point, the wind began to howl.

Pressing ahead we came to a gravel spit covered with gulls and terns lying low. Rounding the spit we punched through a nasty rip, and suddenly found ourselves in a powerful current sweeping us back out to sea, with the headwinds doing the same. We paddled full power but made almost no forward progress. Madly we kept at it, ever-so-slowly creeping ahead. After ten long minutes we pulled out of the strongest current.

Landing ashore in the quiet lee of some dunes we were immediately covered with blackflies in their hundreds. But getting rid of them was a simple matter of stepping back out into the wind, which blew them all away. Walking back to the spit for a look around, we inadvertently chased away the birds. The beach sparkled with thousands of small seashells and seashell bits. Even the tiniest chip of a shell was smooth and polished, and glowed with a pearly essence.

Amongst the shells Jenny found part of a walrus skull with one tusk. It seemed rather old, as the bone was brittle.

With the boat back on the water, the spray immediately washed its deck of the coating of flies. Paddling vigorously against 20-knot headwinds, we crept along the coastline, which now wrapped back toward the south, then west.

Eventually running out of steam we started dragging the boat through the shallows with a short painter. We could not line from shore because the receding tide had exposed gradually sloped and irregular tidal flats. Wading through the water was slow going, and since one person could tow the boat as well as two, I invited Jenny to simply walk along shore. Eventually I tied two 50-foot lines to the boat, one fore and one aft, and lined the boat, not from shore but at least in water less deep.

Meanwhile Jenny scouted the bank above for a possible campsite. With a stronger tent we could have camped almost anywhere along here, but the worrisome conestoga required protection from the wind, which was

Hauling the kayak into stiff and frigid headwinds in Kotzebue Sound

now pushing 25 knots. This was one of those afternoons that required a certain grit (short for grit your teeth) and dogged determination, of which we have experienced many in our journeys. How boring if they were all easy.

After a few hours we stopped and rested. The wind was bitingly cold, but at least had diminished to 15. So we decided to try paddling across a channel that would eventually require crossing anyway. The far beach looked to be three or four miles distant. Unfortunately, in addition to the adverse wind, a wisp of fog was also materializing from across the sound. We paddled away from shore but stayed fairly parallel to it in order to judge our adverse drift. We seemed to be making good progress, so after half an hour we started across the channel.

Much to our surprise, in only 15 minutes we reached shoal water, as indicated by its lack of waves and gathering of gulls wading rather than swimming. I emerged from my cockpit and found the bottom fairly soft. The mud flats appeared to go on forever, so we kept paddling around them to their east. This worked well, and in another 15 minutes were surprised to reach the far shore. We had not been able to see it through the fog, presumably. Then we discovered that it was not the far shore, per se, but a series of raised mud flats resembling islands. These we paddled along, and eventually reached a genuine shore backed by a 50-foot bank. Unable to make out the way ahead, we climbed the bank and saw that the shoreline ahead was very straightforward.

Suddenly again the day's tone changed again. Gone were the fierce headwinds and dashing spray. Now we glided along pleasantly in a 10 knot tailwind. This wind was from the north, since this part of the shoreline of Kotzebue Sound runs generally south.

However, for the remainder of the day we experienced great difficulties making out the terrain ahead. Mirages kept playing tricks on our eyes. Once we thought we were about to run into an island. We landed and climbed the cutbank, and saw very clearly that there was no island, only smooth, continuous coastline. Here the snow bank was melting, and we could have filled our water bottles but were already carrying an ample supply.

We have climbed a rise for a better view of the coast ahead.

The seabirds were prolific and often entertaining, especially as they flew close by in tight formation. Deeper into the sound we saw a seal. But while crossing a shallow bay we were startled by the emergence of some indescribably ugly creature surfacing very near the boat. It was covered in seaweed, and was only a large clump of peat, lying in the shallows.

We climbed another 50-foot bluff to determine our whereabouts, and saw that we had nearly reached the back of the sound. But as the day wore on, we could not connect the visible scenery with that shown on the chart. So we switched on "Geepus" and found that we had come only 10 of the 30 miles to the back of the sound. We were learning not to trust our eyes. What was seen was not necessarily what was. For several hours we had been watching a brilliant white tower of some sort, far out in the sound. This turned out to be a small, circular patch of snow on the distant mountains. The mirage had stretched it vertically and illuminated it.

After paddling across a wide bay, we reached the far bank only to discover it was an island. The first clue was the menagerie of sea birds dwelling there. We had been paddled through shallows most of the day, but the way ahead was now even less deep. And repeatedly we had to land ashore for a slightly higher vantage, to better see where to go. Making our way inside another island, barely fitting between it and what appeared to be the mainland, I turned around and was startled to see that the mainland was miles away. The human eye was proving to be most unreliable - even though the visibility was excellent - and we wondered whether the atmospheric anomalies would have affected a radar screen of a larger vessel in much the same way. Perhaps so.

Reaching a place that appeared to offer good camping, we found the shallows very soft with mud. In fact, to my feet the bottom felt almost like quicksand. So we pressed on, and glided downwind several more miles.

At 10:45 pm we landed, and selected the least boggy place, as indicated by the grasses growing the thickest. Typically the frozen subsoil, or permafrost, prevents the ground water from absorbing in, so it pools the water instead. This is what makes the ground boggy.

Fortunately we had collected tent stakes earlier in the morning and saved them, for small driftwood was absent here. Unfortunately, I could not pound them into the ground because it was so solidly frozen. So we lugged in a few driftwood logs, and secured the tent's stern to them. Then we used the yak's weight to secure the tent's front. Before retiring

A beautiful campsite along the shores of Kotzebue Sound. On the far horizon we catch our first glimpse of ice floes.

we climbed a rise behind camp for a good look around. From here we could see a line of pack ice stretching across the horizon. Ignoring grizzly droppings not far away, we settled into the tent, worn out after a very full day.

Day's Run: 29 n-mi, 11¾ hrs. Camp: 66° 16.087' N, 163° 49.644' W

Day 19: June 23 – Ice floes

Jenny was first to step outside. When I asked what she saw on the horizon, "motus with palm trees" came the reply. While sailing toward a motu from a distance, it looks like bumps. This is what she now saw: bumps. I looked out and verified yesterday's suspicions: pack ice. Perhaps it had not been just another mirage after all. The wind was blowing 10 knots east, directly onshore, but because the water was shallow, the surf was small. So after a hearty breakfast of potatoes and eggs, we set off at 11:00 am feeling like we could have slept another few hours.

Paddling along an extensive high bank laden in snow, we then shortcut across a large river bay, crossing five or six miles of open water. It looked for all the world like we were heading for an island, but the chart and compass suggested we were doing the right thing. Because of mirages, distant coastline can look like empty horizon and mountains like islands.

We joked about writing home and telling of regretfully having missed a televised special about kayaking the Arctic. "We really missed a good program," we lamented. In truth, we were living that program, and enjoying it immensely.

The sky began clearing and continued to do so throughout the day. But as we reached the back of Kotzebue Sound and started heading more eastward, the wind increased our exertion levels and slowed our pace. The water in this southeast corner of the sound - Goodhope Bay - was amazingly shallow. At times we were a quarter mile offshore in only five inches. The benefit to us, however, was that the waves could not build in such shallow water. We took a lot of spray, but no greenies. Finally we found deeper water, then steered for shore and landed near one of the many creeks.

Typically when stepping ashore we begin losing body heat: our lower bodies are no longer protected and insulated by the kayak, and our arm and back muscles are no longer generating metabolic heat. So as we stood on the soft beach and surveyed the coastline ahead, we became deeply chilled. The highest land here was right at high tide line. But even standing at that height, we could see pack ice quite close and headed our way. This was no place to dally.

We rested briefly and warmed ourselves marginally in the sun. Before setting off we noticed a large shoal that would require paddling around. On it stood a number of seagulls. Setting off, Jenny advised me to "keep the seagulls to starboard and the pack ice to port." We thought that that might make a cute title for a story about paddling around Kotzebue Sound.

The pack ice was closing in towards shore, and was threatening to soon block our way. So we paddled with a will for the next hour. Reaching a place where the ice was right against shore, we were relieved to find it was not a continuous mass, but a number of large floes - the largest being about half an acre.

Here was a number of firsts: paddling among floes, seeing the moon for the first time on the trip, finding our first rocks along the shoreline, and deep water for the first time since rounding Cape Espenberg. The seas were becoming rather large, smashing against the ice and jostling the chunks around. The ice was apparently melting fast, because it was breaking apart. It was incredibly unstable, and did not tempt us to land on it – especially when one large piece not far from us toppled with a huge crash.

We turned into a protected bight behind a rocky promontory, and at 6:30 pm landed on a gravel beach, the first gravel we had seen on the trip. Here we found a wonderful place snugly sheltered from the wind in the lee of a bluff. We spread drysuits and life jackets to dry, and enjoyed lunch and a long rest. We were tired and stiff, and would have liked to make camp, but even this was not a good place. The highest gravel for camping was below the spring high line, clearly visible along the shoreline. But any grizzly that happened along would come around the corner and suddenly find itself within yards of our tent. Since sudden surprises like this can be dangerous, we much prefer to camp out in the open.

An hour later we set off again, and found the seas very lumpy with a three or four foot chop rebounding from the rocks. While paddling across the next bay I felt very proud of my sea-going mate. Most would have been terrified of such an exposed crossing. But Jenny seemed totally unaffected. Her confidence was borne of experience, and also of the boat's safety and comfort.

The wind slowly dropped, allowing much better progress. The shoreline was strewn with rocks for many miles, but finally at 9:30 pm we found a place to pull out, in the lee of one of the many points. Caution was in order here, because of the surf and also the rocks. Twenty feet from shore we both got out and stood in 3½ feet of water, and guided the yak in between the larger rocks before picking it up and carrying it to shore. This maneuver was thanks to the neoprene booties, which were working so well this year. For all the walking and wading, still they did not leak.

As we were scouting a tent site, a small airplane flew past not more than 100 feet above. A passenger looked down at us from the back seat. The pilot hailed us with a wing-waggle, then continued toward the Deering airstrip, still about fifteen miles distant. Aside from the native fellow on a motorbike a few days ago near Espenberg River camp, these fliers were the first people we had seen in five days.

Here the flower-studded tundra was exquisitely lush and beautiful. We marveled at our surroundings, and climbing the hillside found a commanding view of the sound, festooned with ice floes. Unfortunately, the largest piece - about the size of several football fields - was directly upwind of us. With some gravity we noticed that the sky to the south was smudged in cirrus and the barometer was dropping like a rock.

Day's Run: 22 n-mi, 8½ hrs. Camp: 66° 05.015' N, 163° 23.094' W

Day 20: June 24 - Deering

Rain fell hard as we slept, but finally eased by late morning. The wind was calm and the sea flat. So in a heavy drizzle we packed, and set off at noon with a boatload of sodden gear.

The beaches were lined with table or refrigerator sized rocks, and even near shore the sea was quite deep. The coastline was emphasized with a number of rocky promontories, and we later learned that one of these was a seal rookery, although we saw no seals at the time. The clouds were low and dark, but our progress was excellent, especially as we were cutting each bay rather than following the shore around it.

Mid afternoon we came to the edge of the pack ice, and found that it extended all the way out to the horizon. We paddled along its edge half a mile toward shore, and there found it to be only a scattering of floes. Through these we easily wended, and for the remainder of the day enjoyed these floes as an ongoing part of the scenery. This section of coast is called Sullivan Bluffs and is a pretty series of golden banks topped in lush, green tundra, with lingering snow banks still in the gullies. We watched the ducks, geese, loons, gulls, even a few puffins.

While paddling directly from Toawlevic Point to Cape Deceit we talked about building a Cruisemobile. This would be a recumbent, peddle-powered "kayak," in which we could remain below decks while peddling into stiff headwinds, perhaps with much less difficulty. We imagined that bicycle wheels could be added for overland travel. We often let our imaginations build such contrivances. Another favorite topic was that of homesteading in the Arctic. As our paddles moved rhythmically and the kayak sliced along quietly, we discussed the challenges of bringing everything needed for the construction of a cabin. The biggest problem would have been heating, as even driftwood was scarce here.

The chart indicated we were approaching the village of Deering, but we could neither see nor hear any evidence of it. This was just as well for the thousands of seabirds nested on the cliffs of Cape Deceit. The water was almost mirror-calm this afternoon, allowing a rare and thrilling opportunity to paddle directly along the base of the cliffs. Perched on every conceivable toehold and sweeping and circling overhead were cormorants, murres, kittiwakes and other gulls, all clamoring and raising a cacophony of protests aimed at the intruders in the kayak.

Cape Deceit was named by Lieutenant Otto Von Kotzebue, a Russian explorer who discovered Kotzebue Sound in 1816. This was only about 50 years before the U.S. purchased Alaska from Russia. As we rounded this cape, the village came into view a couple miles distant. We were about halfway across the bay when an outboard skiff came alongside, and its sole occupant, Jim Moto, stopped for a friendly chat. We talked awhile, then Jim pointed out which building was the store.

At 5:30 pm we landed near the store, and were greeted by half a dozen schoolgirls. The first thing the kids usually asked was, "what's your name?" followed by "where are you going?" and then, "where did you come from?" We would answer their questions, and the kids would either become bored and wander away, or would show even more curiosity. The least inhibited ones would inspect the cockpits, peer into open hatches, and invariably play with the rudder. We were always reluctant to leave the boat untended, so while Jenny went into the store, I stood by the boat enduring the rain in my drysuit and Sou'wester. Jenny bought a few meager groceries, as the shelves were mostly bare, then she proceeded along the shorefront road to the washeteria, while I paddled.

Jim kindly took our water bottles to his house, and filled them with rainwater. The washeteria had closed for the day, so we were not able to launder our clothes, or even get proper showers. But the girls found a shower token in one of the stalls, and offered it to us. The shower produced only a trickle, but still was hot, so did a good job on both of us. This was a blessing, but also a bane for reasons we were later to discover.

Back at the kayak we met a fellow named Rourke, who said he had been here two weeks working on the town's new water and sewer system. A native Alaskan, Rourke was born on his parents homestead, and presently lived with his wife and kids in Fairbanks. He expressed interest in our kayak and journey, saying that he and his wife had done quite a bit of canoeing, their most recent trip being on the Rio Grande. With a glimmer in his eye he spoke of "sneaking" the Grand Canyon, and was interested in the Sea of Cortez. He also talked about an Alaskan foot race in which he participated each year, covering 150 to 250 miles of wild territory. Standing there arms akimbo, body leaning back Alaskan style, he said the Deering area had some of the best wildlife he had seen, mainly moose and caribou. He related also having seen three big grizzlies up one of the creeks a few days earlier. He reassured us that all the bears he had ever encountered had run away from him.

Jim returned with our filled water bottles and did not hesitate to lend us his advise. He was emphatic about not going far from town without a gun. He said flare guns do not always frighten away the bears. He also mentioned having met a Frenchman paddling along this coast six or eight years earlier. Jim's primary interest this time of year was hunting artifacts. A few days ago he had taken his boat up one of the rivers to the west, and found a mammoth tusk. Apparently these were quite valuable and perfectly legal for the natives to collect and sell. He said some other villagers had found a jade hatchet with an ivory handle, and a pair of ivory sunglasses. He figured the pilot of the airplane we had seen was probably looking for ivory. Surprisingly, these planes could land on the beaches.

Everyone we met in Deering was friendly. The town had a nice ambiance and would have made a nice place to base out of, while exploring the interior. Jim invited us to his home for hot chocolates, and Rourke offered us his guest quarters for the night. But we were anxious to make at least a few more miles in such good conditions. So we shoved off at 7:30 pm, two hours after we had landed.

A quick stop for groceries at the friendly village of Deering.

Taking advantage of the calm water, we paddled directly across the bay for the next promontory. We were halfway across the next bay, nearly to Motherwood Point, when the sky started darkening. Anyway we were starting to tire, so in a drizzle we steered for what looked like the best camping, and landed ashore at 11:30 pm. After a bit of searching we found a level area of cobblestones slightly above high water line – which is to say spring high, for the present highs were not reaching that far up the shore.

Here we discovered the disadvantage of having taken the showers. The mosquitoes bit us thoroughly. We had noticed much the same effect earlier in the week, after bathing in a creek. By this we gathered that our skin exuded the B vitamin chemicals that acted as repellant, but that the water washed them off. The perfumes and residues left on the skin from scented soaps are also known for attracting mosquitoes. While on the topic, Chuck, the postmaster at Shishmaref, said that red clothing repels mosquitoes. He admitted it sounded like an old wives' tale, but added enthusiastically, "it really works."

Besides the mosquitoes and light rain, we could not pitch the tent properly. To one end we secured a bundle of the largest driftwood available, and to the other, the kayak. Pulling on the tent's tensioning buckle only dragged the two weights closer together. Thankfully the wind was not blowing. So we settled in, mopped up as best we could, ate a couple of what Jenny referred to as "Jiffy Wonders" (peanut butter on white bread and you wonder what's in them) and fell to sleep.

Day's Run: 31 n-mi, 9½ hrs. Camp: 66° 03.167' N, 162° 12.688' W

Day 21: June 25 – Moose Meadow

The wind was increasing from the north, and we knew that this place would not be safe in a storm. So at 8:37 am we set off, amazed at how quickly the sea could change its disposition. Yesterday we had ridden the expressway, today the Wild Mouse. The seas were only three to four feet, but incredibly lumpy.

After paddling a couple of hours we rounded a headland into a protected bay, and there landed on a stark and meager beach of mud and cobblestone. Cowering in the rain, we knew that we would soon be camping. Because of bears we did not want to cook at that camp, so in the dreary chill Jenny cooked two meals: potatoes and eggs to wolf down right then, and corn spaghetti to eat later. Stretching the legs for a bit of warmth, I found a number of moose tracks, a caribou antler, and an assortment of intriguing mineral specimens.

We set off again and paddled another 45 minutes, and could see in the distance good camping on an expansive grass and willow plateau. A couple of moose were browsing the willow near shore, so we approached them quietly - mostly by coasting downwind, and paddling only when they were not looking. This got us to within 30 yards of them without causing alarm, and this was as close as we dared, for our own safety's sake. They were both very large but lanky after the winter's privation. One had a set of burgeoning antlers, and was shedding much of his winter's fur. Both stood looking at us. We remained motionless, then as we passed by, still drifting, we spoke to them softly and they moseyed up the hill without much concern.

A ways farther we landed ashore at noon, and looked around for the best tent site out of the wind. Finally we decided to pitch on the plateau, atop the grasses. The drizzle was easing, so we spread our things to dry. And thanks to the wind, this they did quickly. How insecure wet gear made us feel, and how nice to have it all dry once again.

After a long nap we busied ourselves with a few projects. Jenny removed the wrist Velcro from my drysuit, which was causing unnecessary chafe. I carved her a new spoon to replace the one lost. She seemed to be feeling a little glum, so I picked a sprig of sweet vetch and placed it on the wall at her side of the tent. She did not notice right away, but when she did, the cheery colors brought a few tears of gratitude.

I was reading when Jenny peered out and saw a small herd of caribou or reindeer coming down the hill. There were about eight of them altogether – including two with large antlers, and two or three young. The wind was blowing directly from us to them, so they soon discovered us and turned back up the hill, not running but not moseying either. Soon they had disappeared from sight. This was all the big game we cared to see in this particular place.

The wind and seas remained boisterous all day, but the sky cleared somewhat. The barometer was steadily recovering after three days of laying low.

Ray's Requirements for Storm Survival: Good tent, good food, and good book. At least the food was not bad, and neither was the book.

Day's Run: 7 n-mi, 3½ hrs. Camp: 66° 02.770' N, 161° 58.011' W

Days 22-24: June 26, 27, 28 - stormbound

For the next three and a half days the storm kept us pinned down. For the initial 36 hours, rain fell steadily. On the second day the wind strengthened to the high thirties and prompted us to relocate the tent a few times. We were reluctant to move too close to the willows, for fear of a bear stumbling upon us unaware. But eventually we were forced to, for the wind protection this brush offered. The protection proved quite good, but still the tent flapped infernally. Jenny lamented that we seemed to be inside a snare drum. She commented that the gusts were rattling the tent so hard that occasionally it sounded like a moose tripping over it. A good tent would have taken the drama out of the situation. A few more paperback novels would have helped also. We had only two books, and both were technical in nature.

We named the place Moose Meadow for the pair that kept hanging around. Essentially ignoring us, they spent most of their time ripping mouthfuls of willow as though there were no tomorrow. But one time we saw them resting on the sunny hillside, looking like a couple of giant mules. Sunny, for indeed the clouds had dispersed. How ironic to see skies of blue and seas of wind-whipped froth. For drinking water we melted snow in a plastic bag, and collected water from a seep, both of which we filtered.

Late afternoon on the 28th the wind started to slacken. Jenny cooked a pot of corn spaghetti and we napped for an hour. The seas were lessening

Three days of high winds kept us shorebound.

just enough to encourage a departure, so at the unlikely hour of 9 pm we set off.

The next stretch of paddling was 10.7 miles across open ocean to Puffin Island. The crossing began in light headwinds, but these calmed about halfway across. Depending on the conditions, ten miles of open water was about our limit. But even this felt like overexposure today with the western sky streaked in cirrus. The next onslaught was obviously on its way.

As we neared Puffin Island, the "unwelcoming committee" came out to discourage our arrival. Seagulls can be extremely protective and territorial, and tended to beleaguer us any time we approached a nesting area too closely.

As we drew near the island, seabirds began pouring off the cliffs by the thousands, and soon the sky was a dizzying spectacle of whirling and reeling wings. True to its name, the island was also home to a great many puffins, and these were a delight to see. Their gaily-patterned heads looked like painted wood - something one might find in a souvenir shop.

Continuing another two and a half miles across open water, we reached Choris Peninsula, and rounding its southwest tip we struggled through a strong rip tide and an adverse current for several hundred yards. Once through that, we followed the coast a few more miles to the isthmus. The time was 1:30 am, now June 29, and was well past bedtime. So we hauled out and made camp on a beautiful, grassy plateau just short of a couple of old, abandoned cabins. The ground was pockmarked in caribou tracks, and nearby was a cliff with a cave at its base. Sleep did not come quickly, and even then we slept only four hours.

June 29, morning stop: Position of camp: 66° 18.208' N, 161° 53.870' W (4½ hours).

Day 25: June 29, continued

The wind was on the rise, so we felt we should be moving along while the moving was good. We departed at 8:15 am and paddled into headwinds and somewhat bumpy seas. The morning was chilly, and the farther we went, the colder. Finally at noon we had to pull out for some much needed warmth. In a drizzle we pitched the tent on a gravel beach facing the tundra-covered bluffs, not far above high tide line. Crawling inside brought the needed warmth, and we slept for a few hours.

June 29, midday stop: 66° 29.957' N, 161° 52.210'W (3¾ hours).

June 29, continued

Greatly warmed and revived, we set off again at 3:20 pm. The wind and seas had diminished considerably, making for easier going. We relaxed and sang a ditty:

It's a long, long, way to Kotzebue

(Around the sound).

It's a long, long way to Kotzebue

(Around the sound).

If you want to get there, you've got to get going,

Cause it's a long, long way to Kotzebue - around the sound.

Second verse:

It's a long, long way to Kotzebue

(Around the sound).

It's a long, long way to Kotzebue

(Around the sound).

If you're getting low on grub, and there's nothing left to chew,

It's a long, long way to Kotzebue - around the sound.

Headless walrus dotted the shore. Altogether we had seen an appalling 70 or 80 from Shishmaref. We had also seen boats of ivory hunters and sometimes even airplanes presumably radioing them with directions.

At one point we happened upon an airplane that had landed on the beach. Because of its nearness to the bluffs, the landing must have white-knuckled any passengers. A ways farther we drew along shore and talked with the pilot and a single passenger, who said they were beachcombing for artifacts. In jest, I asked the pilot if he would care to trade vehicles - his airplane for our kayak. He allowed that if the plane were upside down, he would consider it.

Along this stretch of bluffs we watched a golden eagle, a few peregrine falcons, and some large, beautiful hawks with white and black under wing. These raptors always brought a sense of wildness, and were mesmerizing with their effortless, gliding flight.

Later in the afternoon Jenny lined the boat for an hour, jogging as much as walking. Seated in my cockpit, I felt like a kid in a wagon. Like a hobo in a boxcar, the service was non-existent but at least the ride was free.

We stopped to cook a pot of corn spaghetti, then in a rising northwesterly we plodded along, taking the occasional comber over the bow. For miles the coast was covered in snow, and this blocked the way to the tundra-covered bluffs above. This meant we could not stop and make camp even though the headwinds were 15 and the ride was becoming quite rough. Finally I got out and lined the yak the final mile to the end of the snow patch. There we hauled out at 9:30 pm and pitched the tent on the gravel.

The wind dropped and the mosquitoes responded in droves. But our B-vitamins were still doing a reasonable job of fending them off. I received only one bite, and that was inside my sleeve. Apparently the mosquito had become trapped inside my drysuit as I was putting it on earlier in the day.

Day's Run: 43 n-mi, 14¼ hrs. Camp: 66° 42.153' N, 162° 12.636' W

Day 26: June 30 – Kotzebue

After a restful if brief night, we set off at 4:00 am into light headwinds that gradually increased. For an hour we paddled into a stiff chop, concerned about being waylaid by another storm just short of the town of Kotzebue. But the wind eased and eventually calmed altogether. Cape Blossom was only a smudge on the horizon when we had started, but gradually we made way and were soon straining our necks watching a peregrine on the bluffs towering directly overhead. Three Inupiaq had taken station atop Cape Blossom, and were glassing the expanse of sea with binoculars. We exchanged waves and one hollered down, "seen any beluga?"

The chart depicted shoals extending from the cape for ten miles to Kotzebue. The tide was near spring high, and this apparently worked in our favor because we encountered no shallows. As we drew near a landing in front of the airport, the morning had become very hot and we were looking for shade. Then a cloud passed over and within minutes the temperature dropped, prompting us into our parkas.

We had just landed, at 9:50 am, when a woman stopped to look at the kayak. She introduced herself as Glenda, and said she owned a Klepper. She had worked here in Kotzebue for five years as a nurse, and this morning was checking on her sled dogs before going to church. She gave Jenny a ride the quarter mile into town. Jenny found a room at the Bayside, for a whopping $106 a night.

We paddled the yak along shore to the hotel, unloaded, and stashed it in the weeds alongside the building. After freshening up a bit we enjoyed a hearty breakfast of steak, eggs and pancakes - for $32. Despite the high prices, Kotzebue seemed like a pleasant place, not overly inundated with junk strewn about, nothing like Nome and certainly no comparison with Shishmaref. The tradeoff was that generally the people were amicable but not welling over with friendliness. This was understandable when Glenda told us that several busloads of cruise ship tourists visited daily through the summer.

The sea in the vicinity of Kotzebue was particularly clear, mainly because three enormous rivers empty into the bay, and their outflow washes past this coast. This outwash was clearly indicated by ripples and whorls of current, and at times even rips. We did not check the sea here, but it was probably fresh water rather than saline. Kotzebue itself lies at the tip of a long peninsula, so during the warmer months, boats and planes are the only means of reaching the mainland. To the north across the sound, spectacular mountain ranges punctuated the horizon. These mountains, with their hidden valleys and cold, clear waters, were very alluring to our adventurous spirits.

Day's Run: 18 n-mi, 6 hrs. Camp: 66° 54.25' N, 162° 36.5' W

Day 27: July 1

The post office opened at 9:00 am, and we were there to collect the resupply boxes we had sent from home. To our good fortune we also received the new tent. Right away we spread the groundsheet, and after much head scratching, pushing and tugging on various poles and fistfuls of nylon, we managed to erect the thing. One look inside, and we knew we had something truly grand.

The morning had started out calm, but by the time we had read through our few pieces of mail and scribbled hasty replies, and had packed up our gear, the sound had become white capped. So we asked the hotel proprietor if we could set up camp behind the premises. He gave his permission, but after a while the wind began easing, so we carried gear and boat to the beach and loaded up.

The pile of gear and food seemed mountainous, but with careful packing it all fit neatly into the yak. We were now carrying quite a large supply of food, along with the new tent as well as the old – just in case, and the new waterproof camera in addition to our trusty SLR. As we sat with the boat, several people stopped by and said they had seen us from various airplanes and boats.

I flipped on the aircraft radio and scanned to Kotzebue ATIS. They were reporting wind 190 at 13. The sound was still somewhat white capped, but the wind was easing and seemed to be on a reliable trend. So at 1:20 pm we set off.

On the horizon ahead stood the beautiful Igichuk Hills and Baird Mountains. At first glance they gave the impression of being dusted with snow, but later we realized they were simply above timberline, which was not very high in these parts. And probably the soil itself was light in color.

Except for the background mountains we could see no features along the coast. The Shesualek peninsula, our immediate destination, was apparently very low lying, for we saw nothing of it until within a few miles.

The wind began on the port quarter and gradually swung to fine on the port bow. Fortunately for us, the wind strength diminished as it veered, so we experienced only light headwinds for most of the 7½-mile crossing.

Halfway across I checked our drift with Geepus, imagining that the strong outflow of the three rivers would set us well to the southwest. But this proved not to be, so I continued steering directly ahead by compass.

A ways farther our paddles hit bottom. By chance we had found a bank of shoals. We were not in danger with such a small boat, but it felt strange to be a mile and a half from shore yet in only eight inches of water.

People in Kotzebue had warned us about the seven mile crossing to Shesualek [she-SWOL-ek] Point, saying that the outflows of the three big rivers emptying into the basin can create hazards for small boats.

The sea gradually deepened, then when three quarters of the way across we began seeing strange white dots on the horizon. Later we realized they were wall tents on the shore, and before long we had a whole line of them standing in the distance ahead.

Suddenly we caught sight of riptide on the port horizon. This was bad news, because the current that was causing the rip could also sweep us into it. Redoubling our efforts, we paddled ahead with a will. But our drift was proving minimal, so we paddled alongside the rip for a mile and a half. Finally, half a mile from shore we entered an area of breaking surf that called for some fancy maneuvering to avoid.

In order to proceed along the coast, we had hoped to skirt the line of rip in calmer water between it and shore. But as we drew near shore we saw that the rip extended right onto the beach. Not wanting to be stopped for the day, we paddled into the rip a short ways to test it out. But very quickly it started to overpower the yak, so we turned around and beat a hasty retreat.

We seemed to have little choice but to land on the eastern, quiet side of the rip zone. Standing on the beach and looking at the vast area of roiled and seething water, we could not figure out what was causing it. The currents did not seem pronounced. But to the east the surf was absent, and to the west it was everywhere. This was definitely a rip.

With me at the bow and Jenny at the stern, we waded the boat through the water paralleling the shore, holding on tightly against the onslaught of surf. The bottom sloped steeply to waist depth, then leveled out. But we could not walk on the sloped part because of the dumping surf. So we waded waist-deep, and found the going extremely slow and laborious.

Half an hour of this and Jenny retreated to shore, leaving me struggling ahead. This was just as well, because I found the going no more difficult or unsafe by myself. Jenny was tiring, and understandably felt safer out of the water. The wind had ceased, the day had grown quite warm, and the water was not particularly cold. So I sweated inside my drysuit, all the while swatting at mosquitoes. Several times I splashed my face for the coolness and to rinse away the sweat.

After a long struggle of wading along the shore, we pitched the
tent and waited a few hours for the turn of the 3-inch tide

Forty-five minutes of this and I, too, began to see the futility. So I dragged the boat out, and we both stood there a long while contemplating breaking out through the surf. We tried to hold the boat pointing out to sea enough for me to climb aboard and secure my spray skirt, but the surf had other ideas. The minute either of us let go, the yak swung powerfully in. Reluctantly, we called a temporary halt, and at 4:45 pm pitched the conestoga. At least our wet clothing dried quickly in the hot sun.

July 1, midday stop: 66° 59.674' N, 162° 50.865'W (3½ hours).

July 1, continued

We relaxed in the tent, glad to be out of the mosquitoes. After 2½ hours the rip slackened, so we struck camp and made ready for departure. As we were packing gear bags into the kayak, a fellow from the nearby fish camp stopped by for a friendly chat. In halting English he assured us the surf extended all the way along the coast in front of us. And he welcomed us to camp anywhere around here that we liked.

At 7:15 pm we were ready to go. With careful timing we launched the yak and hastily paddled out past the largest rollers. Then we proceeded west along the coast, happy to be underway once again. For the remainder of the day we paddled into light to medium headwinds, glad to be making at least an afternoon's worth of progress. The sky overhead was streaked with cirrus, the sky away to the south was covered in a greasy smudge, and the mountains to our right were overshadowed by ominous lenticulars. All these warned of the next frontal system, and reminded us once again of the Arctic's volatile climate.

The farther we went, the larger the rollers and heavier the surf, despite light winds. After paddling along an extensive sandbar, obviously backed by a large lagoon not visible from our low vantage, we reached the bar's western end - and the eastern edge of Kilangnak Bluff. Here the swell was no longer breaking so far out, and this told of deeper water inshore. The time was 11:00 pm and we had found a place to land. Before starting in, I reminded Jenny not to merely ride the yak in, but to control it. This had excellent effect, for as we paddled hard between sets, and were caught by a small dump near shore, Jenny braked hard and we both stepped off. However, another wave knocked the paddle from my hand. We both reeled in the dizzying, powerful backwash, but it was Jenny who saved the day by quickly dragging the yak to higher ground. I merely floundered in the surf trying to save my paddle, and in the process another breaker knocked me off my feet. Fortunately by the time I had struggled ashore, Jenny had the situation well under control.

Curiously, the water here was vastly colder than it had been back at the spit. The strip of land was fairly narrow, and behind it stood Aukalak Lagoon, beautiful and serene. High ground was lacking, and the small bluff was steep and covered in thick brush. We figured if a storm moved in, we could paddle across the lagoon to safer ground. So we pitched the new tent. Crawling inside, we found it positively luxurious. It was so roomy that we christened it The Coliseum. This particular tent had seven large-diameter poles, and the feelings of security it imparted were indescribable. No longer would high winds at camp be a constant source of concern.

Day's Run: 20 n-mi, 7¼ hrs. Camp: 67° 03.592' N, 163° 16.058' W

Day 28: July 2

We slept until 1:30 pm, nearly 12 hours. Rain had fallen much of the night, and the wind was out of the south at a boisterous 15 to 20. The seas looked rough, so we were glad to enjoy a day of relaxing in the tent, napping and reading. In fact, its luxury was so pronounced that we did not even feel like venturing outside.

Two fellows drove past on motorbikes, and I happened to be out the second time they went by. One stopped for a chat, and said he lived four miles to the east, and that he was born in the area. He said his relatives all lived at Point Hope. He had seen us paddle by his place yesterday, but thought we had two kayaks because he saw two people. We were well

We could now camp in comfort, even on the exposed beaches.

offshore at the time. I asked if grizzlies frequented the area, and he replied that yes, many, but that they would not be coming down to the coast for another month.

We went back to sleep at 1:30 am (July 3)

Day 29: July 3

We were ravenous as usual, and had brought a good supply of both fresh and dry food. So Jenny volunteered to cook. To avoid cooking odors permeating our new tent, sleeping quilt, and other gear, she moved fifty feet away downwind of camp.

The sky had greased over from horizon to horizon, but the wind was merely wafting at five knots. The day was not the most promising, but we needed to make the best of it. The wind soon veered, and piped up just a bit, so we paddled into headwinds throughout the day. But not to worry, for we were getting into better shape, so were better able to buck the headwinds.

Eventually we rounded Cape Krusenstern. This was a milestone: exiting Kotzebue Sound at long last and turning our bow north, back into the Chukchi Sea. Also we started seeing more seabirds, and fortunately for the walrus population very few headless ones. The coast was low lying due to the presence of a large lagoon behind it. We saw no boats and only a couple of airplanes winging across the sky at a distance. We passed by the occasional cabin or tent cabin, but none seemed occupied.

At 2:10 pm we hauled ashore, and Jenny cooked a reviving batch of corn spaghetti goulash, using leftover ground beef and potatoes from the previous night's dinner. She also made extra-large hot chocolates. The wind was now northwest, and whenever it came from anywhere from west through north it was positively frigid, since it was coming off Siberia or down from the polar ice pack. But by now the sun shone encouragingly, imparting a small measure of physical warmth. The sand showed tracks of bear and the usual 4-wheelers. An hour after arriving, we set off again.

Jenny has keen eyesight and is quick to pick up any movement. She always seems to spot the wildlife first, and this time it was a fox. The creature was trotting along shore searching for something to eat presumably. We also noticed a herd of what looked like muskox grazing on the mountainside. They could have been caribou but seemed too dark and rotund. The wind increased and the chop began throwing us around.

Away to the northwest the sky was smudged in cirrus, so we determined to make the most of what good weather remained.

After the large bowls of hot chocolate at lunch, we required a shore break. In fairly calm water we could kneel in our cockpits, and peel our drysuits far enough for using a bailer. But in rough water such as today's, peeling the drysuits would have been risky. The water was painfully cold and falling into it with drysuits open would have been worse than wearing none, because the suits could have flooded and made re-boarding extremely difficult.

Standing on higher ground we gazed northward at the sight of something truly phenomenal - we knew not what. It was brilliant white and perfectly rectangular. It appeared maybe 50 feet tall and 300 feet long. It looked quite real, but we figured it had to be a mirage. We did not see it again today, even though by the end of the day we had paddled to nearly where our minds said it should be.

The day's final couple of hours were strenuous, owing to increasing headwinds. So we were glad to reach some higher ground at the far end of Kotlik Lagoon. Here we landed and made camp at 6:15 pm.

As with yesterday's landing, today's was made challenging by a three-foot surf dumping suddenly onto the beach and creating a strong backwash. But we were beginning to figure out a few techniques. First and foremost, we fixed our gaze on the shore. The backwash accelerated powerfully seaward, and if we looked at it, it tended to disorient us. Typically I timed our exit carefully by the wave sets, then we paddled shoreward at full power. Just before the bow hit shore, I would brake hard, Jenny would jump out and run to the bow and drag the yak quickly to higher ground. Meanwhile I would exit and assist the last bit. This had to be done quickly to prevent the next onslaught from washing into the cockpits. During our final landing today Jenny's timing was spot on. A second later and a large dumper would have flooded my cockpit. But she deftly snatched the boat away just as the water was crashing down.

The sun was still gleaming so we spread our things to dry on the tundra, while savoring the fragrance of Labrador tea and the myriad, tiny, aromatic and vibrant plants and lichens that made up the rich mosaic of the tundra flora. Each footfall ever so slightly crushed the miniature garden, and another waft of fragrance would be released. We checked a nearby creek and lagoon, but found them to be saline. We also had a peek inside an isolated and newly built trapper's cabin. It featured a wood stove and a selection of canned foods, a table, benches and two bunks.

Back at our campsite we were thankful again for the new tent, since this site was fully exposed to the elements. The extra weight did not seem to be hampering our paddling speed, and while the tent took longer to pitch, it was well worth it.

Day's Run: 34 n-mi, 11 hrs. Camp: 67° 25.755' N, 163° 52.979' W

Day 30: July 4

We set off at 8:30 am into light headwinds that built gradually through the morning. In the distance was what appeared to be barges and machinery. Finally we had come close enough to see that it was some sort of mining operation. And we could also see the strange feature of yesterday. It was a huge building with a white stripe running along its edge. Curiously, the mirage had raised only the white portion above the horizon.

As we approached the operation the seas grew white capped. So rather than be driven ashore directly in front of the terminal, we decided to stop short. Pulling in at 11:00 am we spread things to dry in the warm sun, and attended to a number of repairs. Jenny's left drysuit booty had split a seam and was leaking. This we repaired with a special cement positioned temporarily with adhesive tape. The bulkhead behind my seat had torn loose somewhat from the hull, the fiberglass tape had split in half. Weight applied to my seat forced the hull down and put this joint in tension. I repaired it with a thick bead of silicon. The downhaul rudder cord had frayed nearly in half, so I replaced it with a new cord carried especially for the purpose. Jenny applied a UV protectant to our drysuits' latex seals, hatch cover, cargo hatch gaskets, chart pouch and clear ditty bag. The chart pouch had split a seam, so we repaired that with adhesive tape. Altogether we spent a very productive three hours on this cobbled beach.

July 4, midday stop: 67° 31.547' N, 163° 59.344'W (3 hours).

July 4, continued

The wind slackened somewhat and the seas were only mildly white capped, so we decided to press on. Distances are deceptive in the Arctic because of the clarity of air – thanks to the lack of dust and smog - and especially when one is looking at very large objects such as these huge barges, tugs and conveyor apparatus. Eventually we reached these things and made our way around them, then carried on along the coast. The chop was considerable and the headwinds had become a force to reckon with. Our progress was slow, but at least we were making some.

By late afternoon Jenny was running out of steam, so against her weak protests we landed ashore at 6:45 pm and pitched the coliseum atop a four-foot grass covered cutbank. Behind camp was a long, narrow lagoon, and between it and us was a field of grasses, willows, and wildflowers galore with many that looked and smelled like ramps. Jenny felt remorse at having curtailed our day's progress, but I reassured her that it was the headwinds and chop that had exhausted us and reduced our mileage.

As we were establishing camp, two fellows came by on a 4-wheeler. From them I learned that the heavy apparatus we had paddled past was for a lead and zinc mine, located forty miles inland via its haul road. The mine had been operating for ten years. Like those before them, these fellows wanted to know if we had seen any walrus with ivory. We said we had seen plenty of carcasses, but had not checked for heads. We always tried to ask subtle questions, so as not to offend. We were learning that the walrus were hunted at sea, and when shot they sank. The hunters dropped a buoy, then dragged a grappling hook until snagging the carcass. After decapitation, the body was discarded whereupon it eventually drifted ashore, and the next storm washed it up onto the beach. By now we had seen literally hundreds. Some might have called it slaughtering as opposed to subsistence. People had said it was worse down around Nome, but the body count had been fairly consistent all along our route, at least from Deering.

Sleep was difficult because the sun's heat was coming through the walls of the tent and making it feel more like an oven. That, and the sun's reflection from the sea had roasted our faces the past few days. The tent's interior was also extremely bright during most of the "night." In the lower latitudes, where the sky turns dark on a midsummer's night, one's eyes can rest. But here they must constantly contend with the brightness.

Day's Run: 16 n-mi, 4¾ hrs. Camp: 67° 40.220' N, 164° 19.180' W

Day 31: July 5

By early morning the wind had dropped to a whisper. We stepped outside and walking through the dew-covered grasses kicked up clouds of mosquitoes. They set hard upon us, but our B vitamins were working well.

We set off at 6:15 am and paddled half an hour in calm conditions, stopping briefly after about five miles to collect and filter water from a creek.

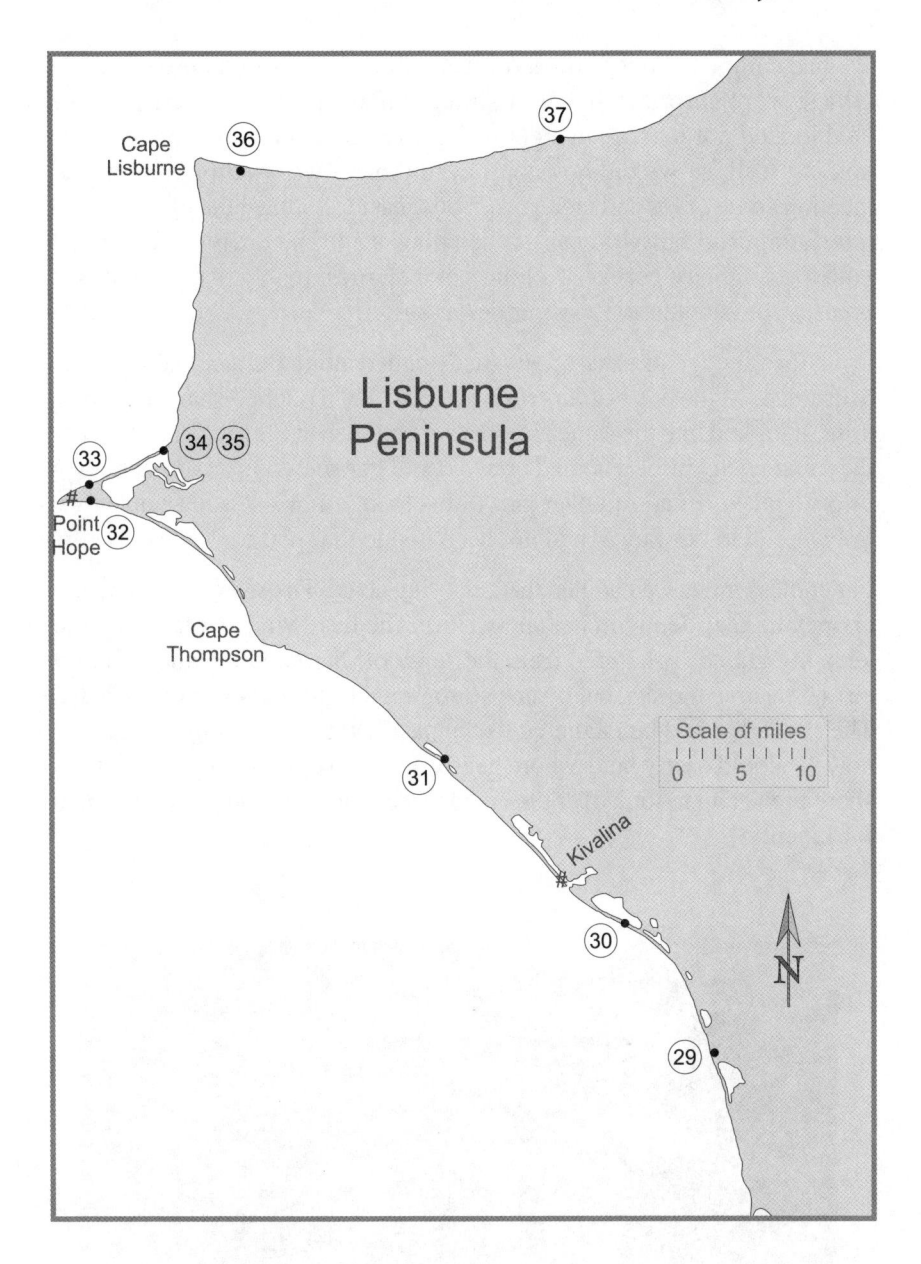

Then the headwinds began to wrinkle the sea. Paddling into headwinds is like riding a bicycle uphill. You go slower while expending a great deal more effort. Eventually the ripples became whitecaps, but after awhile the wind eased, and we paddled most of the day in 5-8 knot headwinds.

We had camped about 8 miles from Kivalina, and as we approached the village were surprised to see it sitting quite low. The highest point of land looked not more than eight feet above sea level. Our supplies were holding well, so we did not stop - even though we would have enjoyed meeting some of the villagers. From our seaside vantage the place looked interesting, and fairly tidy as native villages go. The town was crammed onto the southeast corner of a long sandbar, presumably to catch the best breezes for keeping the mosquitoes at bay.

From the far edge of town a runway extended along the sandbar for quite a distance. At the edge of this runway was a DC3 pitched sharply onto its nose. It looked like the same airplane we had seen at Shishmaref. Possibly the same cocky pilot who had cranked and banked on his approach, then prior to take off had run over part of his load, a stack of soda-pop cases. We were glad our kayak had not been inside that plane.

For endless miles we paddled the low-lying coast. The sea was sufficiently choppy to keep Jenny in her spray skirt. The headwinds were enough to keep my glasses splattered from the spray off her paddle blades. Greasy cirrus smeared the sky, but by late afternoon the clouds began to dissipate. The swell that had beleaguered us the past few days was mitigating, and now we could easily land ashore nearly anywhere. Twice we landed for a shore break and to look over the embankment, and at 2:00 pm we stopped for lunch.

Siku Kayak -- 93

The farther we were proceeding beyond Kotzebue Sound, the clearer the water. It was now a beautiful crystalline blue-green. A couple of porpoise swam past, one at fairly close range. Overhead the usual seabirds wheeled round.

Late afternoon a pair of 4-wheelers came rumbling along the beach, then two motorboats paralleling shore, one of which stopped. The three men were from Kivalina, and looked like something out of a National Geographic magazine, dressed in skins and seated on reindeer skin cushions. One fellow's face-ruff looked like wolverine and was embellished with dangling eagle claws. The fellows were quite friendly. Up here, Jenny usually opens the conversation by asking, "Where are you going?" This is what they usually asked us, so she was simply beating them to it. And it always seemed to work. They were headed for Cape Thompson to look for beluga, and also to gather eggs. They said what kind, but they used a native word we did not recognize. Later we learned that the eggs gathered here were mainly murre.

At 7:00 pm we landed at the first high ground in many miles. Like many beaches before it, this one had a single set of grizzly tracks, fairly fresh. It also had moose tracks. After pitching the coliseum we sat outside for a few minutes reveling in the beauty of the land and seascape. In the distance, green sloped foothills reached up to the De Long Mountains. Around us were lush tundra, lagoons, pristine beach and sparkling sea.

All the beach sand for the past few days had been newly placed, probably by the same storm that had pinned us down at Moose Meadow. Presumably this same storm was also what had bulldozed most of the creeks and lagoon inlets closed. The beaches had the appearance of an extremely high tide, fresh and clean. The tide was only a few inches, so most likely the effects had been caused by a storm surge: the westerly winds blowing so strongly that they press the sea toward land and raise the water's height by several feet.

The mountains inland were named for George De Long, who in 1879 sailed the Jeannette into the polar sea with the intention of freezing in and being carried to the North Pole. Icebound for two years, the vessel ultimately broke up. The crew set out in lifeboats, and some of them reached Siberia's Lena river delta, where the venerable captain and a few others perished of starvation.

Day's Run: 34 n-mi, 12 hrs. Camp: 68° 02.561' N, 165° 24.189' W

Day 32: July 6

Rain fell during the early morning hours. When it ceased, we rose and sponged the tent fly, packed up, and set off at 7:30 am. The winds were light offshore and the sea had calmed considerably, making for ideal paddling. We traveled past a set of hills that reminded us of the three north of Nome. Here in the Telavriak Hills, two muskox were grazing and making their way down the slope. Their dark brown, shaggy bodies and stubby blond legs made identity easy.

Eventually we reached a broad valley called Chariot. This was one of the prettiest we had seen along the coast. It looked like an ideal village site, and even a good place to spend a summer. It had a heartily flowing creek, mountains galore and good access to the sea. It was close to Cape Thompson with its striking limestone cliffs and fabulous seabirds, so no doubt the hunting and fishing here were excellent. In the small valley were four small, run-down cabins, a bit of old machinery, and a few abandoned roads.

Enjoying a 10-knot tailwind we paddled along the sea cliffs of Cape Thompson. This was a spectacular embankment, perhaps a thousand feet high and five miles in length. The bird life was by far the most spectacular yet of the trip. The feathered creatures were staggering in their numbers. The limiting factor of population seemed to be not food but nesting space. On this huge expanse of cliffs was not a single tiny ledge or perch unoccupied. The birds had crammed themselves together practically wing to wing. Cormorants and kittiwakes, puffins with dark orange beaks, and most numerous were the murres, penguin look-alikes in their black tuxedos and contrasting white shirts. In flight these were amusing to watch because they used their webbed feet as rudders and stabilizers. Another bird we did not know at the time was the black guillemot with its striking red feet and touch of white on the wing. The ever-present glaucous gulls spent much of their time harassing the cliff dwellers and trying to raid their nests for eggs and young.

Just for fun we paddled through a pair of impressive arches, something we would not have attempted in a west or southwest wind, or in tumultuous seas. But as we rounded the final set of cliffs the wind became furious. These cliffs seemed to be generating their own weather. Fortunately the blast was from astern, so at times it fairly flung us along. We stopped for a quick shore break, but the heavy cloud cover and piercing wind eliminated any tendency to linger. With the south-southeast wind on our port quarter we made way along an endless line of low-lying coast backed by lagoons one after another. The sensation was that of paddling in a hole, because we could not see anything above the gravel beach. To our left was nothing but ocean, and to our right nothing but beach. We figured we were missing a great deal in terms of viewing the interesting hinterlands.

Eventually we landed at a patch of tundra just short of Aiautak Lagoon, by far the largest along this stretch. We were feeling quite tired, and the day was too cold to linger. Either we had to keep moving or make camp - and indeed this would have been a lovely place for camping on the tundra. Another option would have been to portage the short distance into the lagoon and paddle its flat, calm water. But we could barely make out a couple of faint bumps on the horizon, and thought it might be the village of Point Hope, so we decided to get ourselves a little closer. Rather than risk floundering around in the shallow lagoon, we opted for the open ocean, despite the wind and waves slopping over the decks. Hour after hour we paddled along the gravel beach and progress was good thanks to the quartering tail wind.

Near the ruins of comically named Jabbertown we landed ashore with thoughts of making camp. But here we found nothing but gravel imprinted everywhere with ATV tracks, and from a higher vantage we could see that we were not that far from Point Hope. So we continued ahead.

Several 4-wheelers raced by, and we saw one car with what looked like a tourist family out for a Saturday drive. The car appeared to be experiencing difficulties negotiating the sand and gravel. To us it seemed strange for city people to be out here, probably without emergency food and extra warm clothing.

While setting off from another shore break we nearly swamped the yak. The beach was fairly steep and the surf was pounding. As we were setting up for the launch, a wave took hold of the yak and nearly filled its cockpits. We dragged ashore, and after bailing prepared for another try. This time I instructed Jenny not to linger in the surf, but that when in the water to her knees she was to charge seaward, jump in and start paddling vigorously. So this is what she did, while nearly leaving me on shore. I grabbed my cockpit at the last moment and barely managed to fling myself aboard. And with that we were away.

On the last of our arms we managed the final few miles, then at 6:30 pm landed a quarter mile short of the town on a vast expanse of gravel. Against all hopes at this late hour Jenny trudged into town to see if she could collect our resupply boxes. I busied myself with camp chores, spreading things to dry and pitching the coliseum, no small task when tired. To my surprise, an hour later she returned lugging our two boxes. The postmaster had written on one of them: "QAYAQ People."

Ever industrious, Jenny gathered our clothes and returned to town. She barely made it to the laundromat and shower facility before its closing time. Home again she cooked up a hearty batch of potatoes and eggs, using the frying pan we had placed in the resupply box months ago. Chores finished, or near enough, we fell into a well-earned sleep.

Day's Run: 37 n-mi, 11 hrs. Camp: 68° 20.6' N, 166° 40.5' W

Day 33: July 7

Point Hope had only one store, and it was closed Sundays, along with the washeteria. But most importantly we needed to mail home a few extra things. We were tempted to simply dispose of them, including the expensive but worthless old tent, and to carry on to the post office at Point Lay. But ultimately we decided to accept a forced layover day, waiting for the post office to re-open on Monday at 9:00 am. This switched us off nature's time, where the winds and seas had determined the ebb and flow of our daily lives, and back onto society's time clocks. I normally used my watch as a matter of notation, rather than as a directive, so the switch had us watching the fine weather, feeling that we were essentially wasting what would have been a favorable and light south wind.

Jenny wandered into town for another look around. I was milling about camp when Floyd Oktollik happened along on his 4-wheeler. He was neatly dressed, and said he was on his way to Cape Thompson to collect murre eggs. "About twice the size of chicken eggs," he boasted. For this job he carried a small Styrofoam cooler bungeed to the rear rack of his machine. Floyd expressed interest in our trip, and said he had met a fellow doing much the same a few years back. I asked if that might have been Paul Caffyn from New Zealand. Floyd's face lit up, and he said that yes, he was the one. It seems that Paul had stayed at Floyd's house for the night. Floyd said that the ice was so extensive that Paul had to paddle quite a distance around.

The previous winter Paul and I had corresponded regularly, and from him I had learned much about this coastline. Paul was - and is - one of the world's preeminent sea-kayakers, and a very interesting and congenial fellow to boot. Of his many books, my favorite was *Dreamtime Voyage*, which chronicles his epic circumnavigation of the Australian continent.

Jenny found a hotel restaurant catering mainly to construction workers, and returned to camp with a sack of hamburgers and donuts, virtually the only commodities available that day, she said. They tasted pretty good. In lieu of a shower I settled for a hasty shampoo of beard and hair in a bit of water heated on the stove. Otherwise, we simply relaxed most of the day. In a sense this was just as well, because our arms and bodies were tired from several days of paddling. Even so, we reasoned that nature would have provided plenty of resting time without the post office's help.

We also talked with Willie Nashookpuk, who called himself a whaler. He explained that he worked with his dad's crew, and he told us about the whaling trade. It seems that the warmer current and the wind produced open leads through the ice in early season, and the whales followed these leads on their way north. The hunters waited on the pack ice, and when a whale happened along they set upon it with an explosive harpoon attached to a buoy. After the strike they all set out in their umiaks – paddle-powered prior to the kill so as not to frighten the creatures, but outboards afterwards. These hunters came from far and wide, not only Point Hope, and each crew received a "share" of the take. Mainly they were after the muktuk and meat, which according to Willie was "not bad once you had developed a taste for it." Not particularly good, either, judging by his expression.

Willie owned the umiak resting on the tent frame down the beach a ways and which I had photographed earlier that morning. So I asked him about the interesting lashings that bound these umiaks together. They were extremely tight and I could not imagine the manner of their construction. "With a screwdriver and lots of patience," came the reply. "Each one takes a lot of time."

To save time come Monday morning we decided to portage the sand spit to the lagoon. This would short-cut about six miles of paddling around the point of land. So we broke camp and began lugging our outfit across the gravel, a quarter mile east of town. This required two loads of gear each, and one boat carry together. A lack of strength in our arms and shoulders became ever more apparent, and before long we could not go far with each load. But not to be dissuaded, we managed the traverse in about a dozen stages. Beyond the gravel at about the halfway point, the tundra was carpeted in one of the more magnificent displays of wildflowers imaginable. The flowers were miniature, nothing more than two or three inches high, and clung to the earth for better gathering of the sun's warmth. The entire region was ablaze in color.

We were halfway along the portage when Emma and her husband happened along, riding their 4-wheeler and wondering what we were up to. Together we stood on the colorful tundra, admiring the views both near and far. An elderly couple, they were congenial and easy to chat with. We asked about the whalebones standing upright, not far from where we stood. They said they indicated the fairgrounds where in early June people gathered from all over to attend the festivities.

Finishing the portage in perhaps 1½ hours, although we did not time it, we remade camp near the lagoon's shore, not far from an extensive and newly constructed snow fence. Far into the night we heard kids, presumably, hunting with .22s. Near camp was a dead songbird that would have eaten mosquitoes voraciously. Woe be to any small creature living near an Inupiaq village, although somehow the ground squirrels were abundant.

During the night I awoke and photographed the sun at 3 am. It was one or two diameters above the horizon at its lowest approach. This event does not occur at midnight, as one might expect.

Day's Run: 2-mile portage. Camp: 68° 22.2' N, 166° 40.5' W

Day 34: July 8

Securing camp and carrying a few valuables with us, we set off for town at 8:45 am. Jenny headed for the post office with a box to send home, then the gas station to fill our 2-quart bottles with unleaded gasoline for the stove. A couple of telephone calls and a run through the grocery store completed her chores. I went directly for a long-overdue shower, and to collect drinking water. The shower was divine, but what surprised me was the difficulty of carrying the measly 2½ gallon water jug back to camp. Time and again I had to stop and switch hands. How unlikely to think that I was paddling hundreds of miles along this far-flung coast. And how I hoped the strength sapped from arms and shoulders would return before our imminent departure. But I had come to realize that the key ingredient for such a journey was not, in fact, great physical strength. That tended to evanesce in a few weeks of such prodigious exercise. Rather, the key ingredient was a pleasant and positive outlook, which in turn brought great enjoyment and equal determination.

Reaching camp I dismantled the tent, shifted our gear to water's edge, scooted the kayak carefully there, and was loading when Jenny returned. Carrying an armload of groceries she was wincing in pain of the lower back. Dehydration and the exertions of the portage had taken their toll on us both. She took a couple of aspirin and we both drank large quantities of water. Soon we were packed and ready to go, this at 10:30 am.

The wind had switched during the night from south to north, so our trip across the surprisingly deep lagoon was into steady 5 to 10 knot headwinds.

Eventually we reached the far shore and found protected water in its lee. After paddling along the shore a ways in winds fine on the port bow, we landed. I removed my drysuit, put on sandals, and started lining the boat as Jenny sat in my cockpit steering leisurely with her feet on the rudder peddles. Soon we reached the end of the bar, so together paddled across the gap to the far shore.

Once again I lined, and went for a long ways until eventually the ground became too soft for favorable progress. My first clue was that Jenny was easily keeping up with me while paddling the kayak solo. Anyway we had reached Sinuk Pass, the lagoon's only entrance, and here a strong current flowed out. This outflow was due mainly to the Kupuk River, which empties into the lagoon. Together we paddled across the channel and landed on the far shore to assess the situation. Outside the entrance, the surf was positively pounding the shore, ironically since the winds were only about eight knots at this stage. But away to the west we could see that both the ocean and lagoon were festooned in gnarly whitecaps.

The sea was so rough that we figured we had better hold off, so we paddled back into the lagoon. About then the wind reached us, and I resumed lining the boat, this time pulling in a concerted effort to reach camp before the onset of what promised to be a genuine blow. The shoreline was deeply indented at regular intervals, so a few times Jenny paddled point-to-point a few dozen yards while I walked the longer way around.

After a long haul we reached the lagoon's northernmost terminus, and dragged the yak out of the water. The wind was beginning to howl, and the seas had grown distressingly rough. We were glad we had not tried to tackle them.

We selected a site on the gravel and spent the next hour and 20 minutes pitching the tent. Before we could safely raise it, we had to secure its perimeter with huge rocks. Even then, the powerful wind made raising the tent very difficult. Once erect, however, we had an outstanding shelter. Crawling inside was almost like entering a cabin, so great were the feelings of security.

Day's Run: 10 n-mi, 6 hrs. Camp: 68° 26.282' N, 166° 19.967' W

Day 35: July 9

During the night the wind increased with a vengeance. The tent remained secure, but clattered cacophonously and in the heavier gusts it wailed and shrieked. We pondered the ignominy of finding ourselves stormbound one day after having been post office-bound. But at least we were back on nature's terms, and resolved to try harder to anticipate and minimize the inevitable post office downtimes.

Bundled well and carrying shotgun and flare gun, we enjoyed a long walk. Like the regions we had explored in previous days, this one was pristine and strikingly beautiful. To our north, a green carpet of tundra sloped gently up to a high plateau.

From the heights we looked back down at our bright orange tent and golden kevlar kayak – our insignificant intrusion on the great sweep of gravel coastline.

The region held much evidence of the past, both recent and more distant. On the hillside overlooking the sea was a commemorative ring of sacred stones embellished with a few plastic flowers. On the beach was an abandoned fish camp with its timbers lying among scattered debris. All along the beach were bones of whale, timbers of ships, and even a few antique shoes. We also found a nice creek fed mainly by a large snowbank, as well as a more protected camping place in a nearby small valley to which we could relocate should the tempest increase.

Back in the tent we spent the day reading and resting, while casting occasional glances seaward and noting the appalling size and power of the waves. A hundred yards from camp, a party of hunters had butchered a moose, and left its bones to be picked over, at the moment by a hungry raven and a few determined gulls. The adjacent hillside was pockmarked in ground squirrel burrows. We saw no squirrels, but did see what appeared to be a surprisingly large marmot. Marmots are unlikely this far north, so exactly what type of animal it was, we were not sure.

The tent anchored with hundreds of pounds of rocks. The wind blew so fiercely that it stretched the windward panels.

The wind kept strengthening, so I fortified the tent's snow skirt with sand and gravel. To my amazement Jenny somehow managed to cook lunch behind a few boards erected as a wind break. She spread her galley on one board, and unfortunately only after I had photographed her did she settle on the idea of covering each item with a sizeable rock to prevent it from blowing away. In order to sip our hot drinks we had to cup our hands tightly over them to prevent the liquid from blowing away. Also, I found to my great disgust that man does not pee while standing in a strong wind - facing any direction whatsoever. Jenny said she experienced the same problem while stooping. Better to use the bailer inside the tent, we agreed.

Day 36: July 10

By morning the wind was letting up, but the surf was yet too large for a safe departure. So we idled about for a few hours, enjoying a hearty breakfast. Then at 11:00 am all seemed well, so we loaded up and broke through the surf without difficulty.

For the next several hours the wind was variable. Sometimes it came from behind, sometimes from ahead - depending on which bluffs were fanning it in our direction.

Little did we suspect, when setting out, that the day would be one of the more awe-inspiring in all our sea-going experience. The coastline was stupendous, with high bluffs and cliffs rising to 1,200 feet, interspersed with broad, green valleys each with its own sparkling creek running cheerily to the sea. Each point or cliff seemed to have its own personality. Often they differed in the type of rock comprising them. And as a general rule, where the cliffs were limestone they were covered with birds crammed together on every ledge. We saw many of what we now thought were guillemots – the smallish black birds with red feet and white patches on the wings. We also saw murres, puffins, cormorants, and a type new to us - the crested auklet with a tuft on its snout.

Also we saw more animals in this one day than we had on the entire trip thus far. First came grizzly #1 ambling along a gravel beach. We were cutting the bay at the time and were quite far offshore. Even so, the bear seemed to pay us close attention. Next was a small flock of Dall sheep high on a rise overlooking the sea. Then a bald eagle, then bears #2 & 3, which appeared to be a mother and her yearling. We were closer inshore this time, and at the very sight of us the youngster headed inland with a will, sometimes running. The sow merely climbed a 20-foot rise and plopped herself down on the tundra. From that comfortable vantage she watched us paddle past as though we were the day's entertainment. But when we stopped for photographs she reluctantly rose to her feet and ambled massively away after her youngster. This was encouraging, seeing these enormous animals tending to move away from us.

Near Cape Lisburne were half a dozen muskox, again on a rise overlooking the water. This was the closest we had been to this type of animal, and we enjoyed watching them swagger about like sultans in their stately robes.

Halfway through the day the wind calmed to nearly nothing. The water flattened and became a transparent emerald green, which seemed to complement the green tundra and blue sky, and sometimes the colorful cliffs. Otherwise the shore consisted of the familiar gently-sloped gravel beaches. We paddled quietly, with only the sound of the blades dipping in unison, the slosh of water as the blades pulled through, and the tinkle of drips being shed as the opposite paddle blade drew forward. The sea was so calm that the hydrodynamics of the blade strokes and the eddies they created became a sort of mesmerizing mantra. Then, what started as a sighting of one, or two, or a few, became a mass of dead sea life: something had recently killed a great many jellyfish. Scores of them were floating on the surface.

The farther north we traveled, the more the hills were losing their vegetation. The tundra line was lowering, and the nearer we drew to Cape Lisburne, the more the hills consisted of bare dirt and rock. Also, the more impressive were the cliffs, and the more seabirds they harbored. What a thrill to paddle among so many birds wheeling around, and squawking from the nearby cliffs. The scene bustled with life.

Three times we came upon a pair of squabbling murres. One haggling duo was so absorbed in the fighting that they failed to notice our approach. We steered close, and by mistake nearly ran over them with the bow. I slapped my paddle blade against the water to break up their bickering. One of them dove, and swam beneath the yak like a torpedo, leaving us very impressed with its underwater agility. The other performed the typical murre-hovercraft routine, flapping across the water in a desperate but doomed attempt at take off. Sometimes these birds took to flight easily from the water, but usually they struggled across the surface for a full hundred yards or more before barely taking flight or giving up. They were equally at home under the water as above it, so we guessed that their takeoff ability depended on how much food they had recently eaten, and was now acting as unfavorable ballast.

We were truly blessed with near-calm conditions for rounding Cape Lisburne. Even so, this stupendous cape seemed to create its own wind and seas out of nowhere. And no doubt the currents could produce a deep rip. Suddenly the seas become extremely unsettling, with waves to three and four feet smashing into the cliffs and rebounding back. An icy wind freshened in our faces and we knew that this would certainly be no place for a capsize. Landing anywhere ashore here, one might as well have been on the backside of the moon.

Once we had rounded the great cape, the seas began to settle. The air reeked with guano, and the sea became a turgid, milky brown-green. On a hill high overhead was the dome of an Air Force station, and ahead was the station itself, with its runway and many large buildings, fuel tanks, and so forth. We saw no one walking about, and wondered whether anyone noticed us.

Here a fox came trotting along the beach, and hid behind a boulder as we drew near. A ways farther we noticed a colony of ground squirrels. These land creatures, combined with the uncountable thousands of seabirds, all made for a most interesting day.

Feeling exhausted, at 9:00 pm we landed ashore at the far end of the installation, near a large duck pond. Here we miscalculated the size of the surf and took a breaker into my cockpit. After hauling the yak out, we bailed and sponged the bilge, then looked for a place to camp. Something smelled vaguely like sewer, so we gave that place a miss, and continued 75 yards farther along shore. Finding a suitable area of sand and gravel, I pitched the coliseum while Jenny lugged bags of gear to camp. Then together we carried the boat.

For safety reasons we always placed the kayak just a few feet from the tent, then with a length of cord tied the two together. Both items were essential to our welfare, so both merited looking after. Many sea kayakers and canoeists have lost their boats in the night when the water rose unexpectedly. We secured the yak to our tent not to anchor it, but merely to warn us of any problems. Also, small boats are commonly damaged by heavy gusts tumbling them across the ground. We always placed heavy weights in the yak – bags of food and/or large rocks - and in very strong wind we pointed its bow into the wind.

Of special note, from our previous camp we had seen very little evidence of Point Hope Inupiaq, and for the first time in nearly a month, no headless walrus.

Day's Run: 34 n-mi, 10 hrs. Camp: 68° 52.472' N, 166° 03.810' W

Day 37: July 11

Sounds of wind encouraged us to sleep in. But for nothing, because that wind turned out to be blowing offshore. Jenny made a delicious breakfast of pancakes and steaming cuppas, while ignoring hordes of mosquitoes mainly by keeping her face into the wind and allowing the bugs to collect harmlessly on the back of her parka.

We paddled in the offshore breeze, initially, but the farther we went, the more it came from any direction, depending on which bluffs or cliffs we were traveling in the lee of. For a while the wind was on the nose, and I was considering getting out and lining - until bear #4 came lumbering along. This bear was immature and eager to get at us, even wading out into the water. The encounter was most unsettling.

The going was a bit arduous due to yesterday's fatigue. But we had to keep going past endless bluffs of mud and soft rocks, because possible pullouts were few. At times we paddled in tailwinds, where the gusts would send the yak scudding along. Sometimes the wind was on the beam, requiring us to crab heavily toward shore. The boat had a high lateral slip factor, due to its fairly flat bottom, and while this added greatly to stability in heavy cross-seas, it did require a little more steering input.

We stopped at a nice creek to filter drinking water, but the mosquitoes prevented our lingering. Later, we stopped for a shore break on a sandbar backed by a lagoon. Bear tracks were everywhere, and two main bear trails appeared heavily traveled.

Next we pulled into an alcove with the intention of stopping, where a small valley and its creek met the sea. A flock of kittiwakes was on shore, and surely, we imagined, they would keep well away from any bear. It looked like a good place to camp, and we were heading in when we noticed bears #5 & 6 excavating ground squirrel dens. At the sight of us, one bolted and ran inland. The other looked at us a while, then lay down and rolled over onto its back. It stayed that way for as long as we could see it, as we paddled determinedly away.

A mile further along we reached another possible pull out, and landed ashore. Bear tracks were again well in evidence, some disconcertingly fresh. We needed a good meal, so while I stood by with shotgun close at hand, Jenny cooked corn spaghetti and we ate hastily. The entire dinner stop required only half an hour.

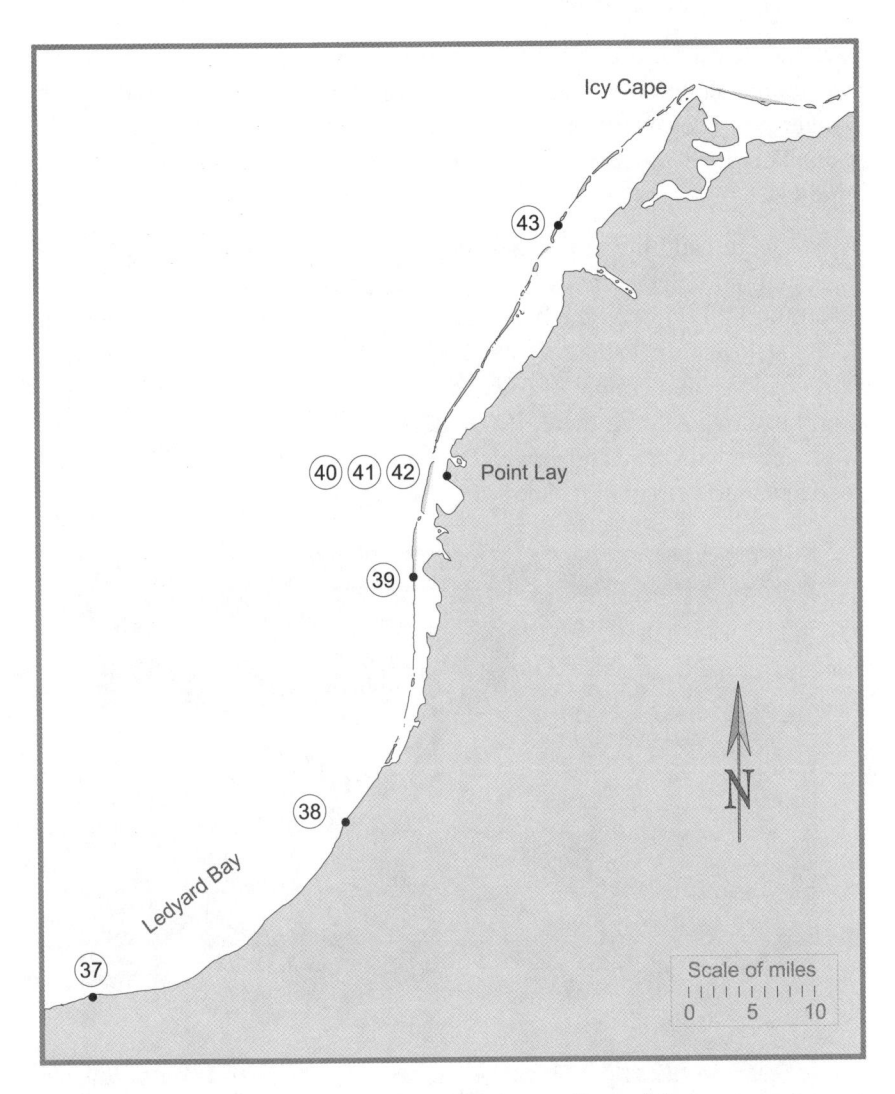

Bear #7 was one of the largest grizzlies we had ever seen. It lumbered unwaveringly along the coast heading south, toward us. We veered offshore, and the bear glanced at us periodically but otherwise paid us little heed. When we had passed each other, it turned and looked back at us. But when we reached the upwind position, it suddenly caught our scent and bounded fearfully away. This reaction was interesting. A bear's sight must be poor, but its sense of smell acute. Perhaps when this one saw and heard us, it did not realize that we were people. But our smell was unmistakable. Inupiaq had told us that the old bears were the least dangerous. They were old because they had learned to fear and avoid man. This bear appeared quite old, and was even limping on its right hind leg.

As we were paddling along, headed toward Cape Sabine, Jenny looked back and mumbled something. I turned and saw that she had discovered a walrus skull lying on the beach - complete with long tusks. We landed Jenny ashore to investigate. The skull was lying on the gravel, partially buried and with a couple of rocks pressed against it, as though a recent storm had deposited it there. It was devoid of flesh, and the skull cavity was packed with sand and gravel. Despite its great weight and size, Jenny loaded it into her cockpit. Soon she had nicknamed it "Hermie."

As the evening wore on, the wind dropped to a whisper and the mosquitoes came out in droves. A solitary caribou stood on the edge of the bluff. It appeared to be in agony over the bugs, shaking itself, and dashing madly one way then another. But when it caught sight of us, it forgot about the bugs and trotted up the hill and away.

Nearly to Cape Sabine I landed ashore to scout the area for a campsite. The place looked like the bears had recently held a convention. The tracks were so numerous that I decided we should move on.

In another mile I landed again, this time at 10:00 pm. Here the tracks were also present, but not in such disconcerting numbers. This was near an old cabin, and a primitive sod dwelling dug into the earth with standing poles all around.

The mosquitoes had been pestering us nearly all day while paddling. Even when far offshore they would fly out to us. Finally I had donned a head net and this worked well. But here on this beach they were something phenomenal - a continual cloud droning around us. We pitched the tent without shedding our drysuits.

We had been trying to combat the bugs with B vitamins. Initially this had worked fairly well at one tablet per day. But as the weeks passed, we found the need to double the dosage for the same results. A few days ago we were up to three pills a day, and even then the mosquitoes were starting to break through our defenses. Our bodies were beginning to reject the "vitamin" intake, as indicated by nausea and a tendency toward seasickness. Our bodies also reeked - possibly also because we were spending long hours sealed inside the drysuits while often sweating a great deal. Today we stopped taking the vitamins, and the next day we started feeling much better. From here we were determined to make good use of the headnets and mosquito-proof shell clothing, along with a few drops of repellent on our hands if needed.

Day's Run: 32 n-mi, 11½ hrs. Camp: 68° 54.796' N, 164° 37.932' W

Day 38: July 12

We rose a little earlier than usual with the feeling that we needed to minimize our time in this bear territory. Braving a storm of mosquitoes

118 -- *Siku Kayak*

we withdrew from the coliseum, quickly packed the yak, and set off at 8:30 am. Fifteen minutes later we encountered bear #8 tramping briskly along the beach toward where we had camped. It paid us no heed until directly downwind. Like the previous one, this big grizzly suddenly bolted into the hills.

The wind was light offshore and the glaring sun reflected off the water directly ahead. Bears came along one after another. A mother and two yearlings were feeding on a submerged carcass. The sow ran away with one yearling dutifully following. The second yearling continued feeding. The distraught mother stood upright on hind legs trying to judge our danger. Reluctantly, she returned to the shore to collect her oblivious offspring, which got the message this time. Together all three trundled away. As they climbed the hill, there came a fourth bear, a large adult. All moved away and out of sight. These were numbers 9 through 12.

With such a reaction we felt more at ease about traveling through this bear country. But the next encounter changed all that. It was an immature adult, quite large and aggressive. It came railroading along the beach, and taking one look at us, it wanted to rip us to shreds. It stood on hind legs knee deep in water, then reversed its direction of travel and followed us, sometimes wading out to get closer. Each bear seemed to have its own personality, and we thought that if one like this wandered into camp, the fun would be over.

Behind bear #13 were three others, #14 through 16, and by then we were far offshore and did not test their reactions. None seemed aggressive;

they were hurrying along, apparently trying to keep up with the first one. Altogether today we saw 14, which brought the trip total to 21.

The day's final bear sighting came as a surprise. We had not seen any for a while, and had been paddling much of the day when we decided to land and cook a meal. We stopped in front of what looked like an old mining concern, just north of the tower at Cape Beaufort. We were both feeling extremely leery, so checked the area very carefully. "Is that a bear over there?" Jenny asked. "No, just another barrel" I replied. We had been seeing these "Alaska Brown Barrels" scattered all along the coast. They were nothing but abandoned 55-gallon oil drums. We were about to start cooking when we both looked up and saw this particular "barrel" heading toward us. The lunch quickly became a launch – and our fastest one ever.

Perhaps not noticing us, the bear headed northeast along the coast, climbed a rise to the top of a bluff, and continued in the same direction as we, at about the same speed. Curiously, of the 21 bears we had seen in the past three days, this was the only one traveling in our direction. After ten or fifteen minutes it found something of interest and was soon left far behind. We were feeling a bit distraught with it all, but fortunately saw no more, and in a few more hours our nerves had settled.

The temperature was extraordinarily warm, with winds light to calm all day. We wore our dry suits to the waist only. Above them we wore mosquito jackets and head nets. The mosquitoes were having a field day, with their nemesis the wind on brief holiday. They buzzed around relentlessly.

A whale broke the surface 30 feet from the yak. It was small and grey, had no dorsal fin, and was about the size of a beluga although we could not quite identify it for certain. We also saw a few seals.

This area is summer home to geese, and we saw numerous gaggles of what looked like brant, each with a dozen or two goslings. The adults were extremely protective of their young, not flying away and leaving them. Paddling vigorously, the young could manage about two knots, but as we drew near they landed ashore and ran along the beach at about 3 knots - which was about our usual paddling speed. During the first encounter we were very sorry to cause them concern, but we could not get around them. For a long ways they kept just ahead of us. Eventually we steered offshore, and finally they turned from the beach and climbed the hillside. The day's final batch comprised about a dozen gaggles, each accompanied by three to six adults. We approached some fairly close, and were amazed at the staunch efforts of the adults to protect their young, even at their own peril. They would run along the beach behind the youngsters, while holding out their wings to distract us. Sometimes they would fly, but always two or three remained with the goslings, herding them away from danger.

Typically these creatures would run along the beach for a great long ways, a mile or even more, and only then would they relent and head up the bank – which is when they easily shook us. Presumably they feared going inland because of the fox. But as we happened upon one particular gosling and two adults, a different scenario evolved. These two adults were running ahead of the little gosling, rather than behind it. All of a sudden junior quit following them and headed up the hill of its own volition. That solved the problem immediately. It was a good lesson in thinking for oneself.

Along this stretch we often heard a deep rumbling of what sounded like an engine. We could see nothing, nor could we smell diesel fuel in the air. It could have been a ship patrolling back and forth just over the horizon, which for us was only about three miles away. Or it could have been a submarine. Other than that we had no ideas.

Late afternoon we stopped on a thin strip of rocky beach to cook a meal. I stood guard while Jenny cooked. The mosquitoes were so intense that we stowed the lidded food bowls in our cockpits and put back out to sea. The entire stop took 20 minutes. Half an hour later we caught a light breeze, enough to thin the mosquitoes somewhat, and were finally able to enjoy our spaghetti. To manage this we did not remove our headnets or even peel them away from our faces. Such would have been an open invitation. Instead we shoveled spoonfuls of food up behind the netting, from the chest or neck area to our eager mouths.

The late evening was exceptionally warm, with temperatures soaring into the 70's, we guessed. But the sun's intensity coupled with our suffocating mosquito clothing and lack of refreshing wind made us sweat. At times the sea was oily and the air thick and stagnant. Curiously, even the sea did not feel terribly cold. This I noticed while washing my spoon. I could hold my hand in the water for quite some while without the usual numbing intensity. Also, the land harbored very few snow banks. Three calm days in a row seemed quite unusual, and because of the bugs forcing us to wear protective clothing, we were finding these still days as challenging for making miles as the frisky ones.

At 8:30 pm we landed to the south of a stagnant, saline creek, and camped on a gravel plateau just north of a weathered survey panel.

Outside the mosquitos whined unceasingly, but we had learned not to smash them on our clothing or tent. In such great numbers, dead mosquitoes create a powerful stench that smells fishy and would even more readily attract bears. Unfortunately this meant that I could not use my mosquitolator. This was a very simple device of my own invention, used on previous trips more for amusement (revenge) but also highly effective.

The mosquilator is patent pending - just kidding - but I will divulge the details. It consists of nothing more than a rubber band. One stretches it from the index finger, points it at the mosquito in question, and lets fly. The mass of a mosquito is nothing compared with that of the rubber band, and if the aim is even marginally accurate the rubber band wins every time. One advantage of the system is that the mosquito does not need to be inside the tent. It can be sitting on the outside. As long as it is touching the fabric, and as long as the rubber band slams into that fabric somewhere nearby, the mosquito is a goner.

In heavily concentrated bugs, using the mosquilator is like trying to dig a hole in the water. Even so, it is quite fun on an individual basis, at least for those of us who enjoy fighting back once in a while. Jenny could not be bothered.

Day's Run: 34 n-mi, 12 hrs. Camp: 69° 11.612' N, 163° 27.551' W

While asleep, we used our drysuits as "scarecrows" to help ward off the bears.

Day 39: July 13

Rain during the night prompted me to dash outside and take down our drysuit scarecrows. These we typically hung on driftwood poles, arms extended, in hopes that they would ward off – not evil spirits - but bears.

Mid-morning the rain stopped, so we sponged the tent's exterior, broke camp and set off at 8:45 am. The wind was blowing 5-8 SW, giving us a quartering tailwind and choppy seas. The coastline was low lying, and even more so once we reached the Kasegaluk Lagoon. The finest feature in this area was its lack of grizzlies, although we did see one set of tracks while landing for a look at a very large set of caribou antlers left by a hunting party.

As the morning wore on, the wind piped up and eventually had us bounding among whitecaps with quartering seas slewing the yak's stern around. The rudder seemed less effective in these conditions because the tops of the waves were moving ahead, so that they actually reversed the flow over the rudder. A keel or a skeg would have acted in the same way, increasing the risk of a broach rather than decreasing it.

All along the way we saw whale vertebrae and skulls, and plenty of driftwood. How ironic to find large tree trunks and branches, and we guessed they had drifted northward in the current. Yesterday we had even seen a creosote-treated power pole lying on one beach.

Reaching the first entrance to the lagoon, we experienced a few tense moments getting across. In places the water was breaking, in other places it was very shallow.

Still on the outside, two or three miles farther we reached Naokok Pass, and by then we were looking for relief from the heavy seas, and even more importantly for safe access to shore. We entered the pass thankfully on an in-going tide. Had it been out-going, the challenges would have been considerable, mainly as the wind had veered to west and was blowing about 15. Pulling around the corner we found calm water, and paddled another quarter mile to a nice grassy landing at 2:00 pm.

Jenny prepared to cook lunch while I scouted around. I found a wooden box which, when stood upright and open to one side, made a perfect wind shelter for her stove. Also I found a large whale vertebra and lugged it back for use as a campstool.

After a reviving lunch of fried potatoes, eggs and cheese, finished off with a sumptuous pan of baked scones, we wandered around for a short while to stretch the legs and admire the glorious wildflowers. Here the species were so numerous that they would have filled many pages in a book.

For the next hour we tried to navigate among muddy shoals, working our way along the edge of the lagoon, sometimes pushing, sometimes paddling, and often with the hull scraping bottom. The wind was still strong, but at least here in the lagoon, close to the windward sandbar, the waves were not very rough. At one point we decided to go around a certain bank, and reaching its far side we had to work hard to regain the shore while paddling into very stiff headwinds. Eventually we broke past the shoals and followed the inside of the lagoon bar, staying close to shore for its protection from the wind. The fog had moved in, and now the wind was icy cold. The contrast between yesterday's weather and today's was remarkable, and a good reminder not to take the Arctic's moods for granted.

We were reluctant to proceed too far, for fear of losing high ground. "High" being about 8 or 10 feet above sea level. So we stopped at 6:00 pm just short of the latitude of Sitkok Point across the lagoon, and about five miles short of Kukpouruk Pass. Once again we were thankful for the coliseum and its welcome shelter and warmth.

We wandered to the sea side for a look at the imposing conditions. To the Arctic creatures the day was simply another windy one. But to us sea kayakers, whose focus tends to be on the wind strength and the resultant sea state, the conditions were gnarly. In fact, the sea was agitated and unwelcoming, the wind relentless and cold, and the surf loud and hammering. We turned from this discordant scene and instead combed the beach, collecting a few pieces of driftwood for use at camp.

Day's Run: 25 n-mi, 9 hrs. Camp: 69° 34.613' N, 163° 08.488' W

Day 40: July 14 – Point Lay

Awaking to the pattering of rain, we turned back in. For after all, we were in no hurry to reach the village of Point Lay - 10½ miles farther on - on a Sunday when its post office would be closed. The wind had greatly reduced, and by the deafening silence we knew that the surf was no longer smashing the beach with such violence. We visited the outside shore and could plainly see a large pan of ice lying half mile offshore to the northwest. Strangely, 15 minutes later it disappeared. We knew that a continuous west wind like that of yesterday could bring the pack ice back to shore and block our way, so we were glad that this spell of west wind had lasted only one day.

We studied the area for tracks and found one set of bear tracks, fairly recent, as well as those of fox, caribou, and the usual menagerie of seabirds and ducks. We also found two nests made of grass, both unoccupied. The tundra flowers were dramatic, as usual. One variety we had not seen before. We dubbed it the "Arctic Chili Pepper," for its long and narrow red seedpods.

Relaxing inside the tent, we waited out another period of rain. When it eased we packed up and set off at 1:30 pm.

The wind was now blowing south-southeast at 5-8. This helped us along, but it also gave some concern. The lagoon was already fairly lumpy, and increasing wind might prevent our crossing to the mainland. Nor did we even know the village's true whereabouts. The map depicted it on the outer bank, but we had heard it had been moved to the mainland.

The day was quite chilly, and the sky completely clouded over with some fog hanging low in the distance. The land itself was low lying and the horizon essentially empty. We could vaguely see the radar dome of the DEW station at Point Lay, so generally steered for it, while keeping well away from shore and its possibility of shoals.

A mile past the lagoon entrance we headed across the vast expanse of lagoon, steering for the radar tower. For an hour we paddled with a will, and finally came within range of the radar installation, and what was now obviously the village.

The village stood on a 50-foot embankment, and camping options in this vicinity were decidedly lacking. We checked one low grassy area but found it to be boggy. Paddling to the other end of town, we climbed the embankment to the outskirts, but the tundra here was too hummocky for camping. So we continued along shore and pulled out at the boat launch, of all places, at 4:30 pm.

Rain had been falling all afternoon, and in a light rain we pitched the tent on the gravel amid a number of outboard skiffs. A family came along on a 4-wheeler, which they then used to push their boat into the water. We tried to offer a hand, but were of little help. After we had pitched the tent, they returned and generously offered us a salmon from their net, which we graciously declined because we knew it would be dear to them.

Jenny wandered into town while I held down the fort – literally because we had not yet gone to the trouble of locating tent pegs from among the scant driftwood. Within a few blocks she met four teenage girls, two of whom had been on the 4-wheeler back at the boat landing. Jenny asked them for directions to the store, and from that point had her own guides. The store had closed for the day, but the school was open for the construction crews, and that is where the girls took Jenny to place a phone call.

Jenny filled her water jug at the school kitchen's sink, then the two girls, Christina and Alicia, accompanied her back to the tent. They sat around talking with us awhile. They said they had pulled nine fish from their family's net today.

Day's Run: 11 n-mi, 3 hrs. Camp: 69° 44.938' N, 163° 00.515' W

Days 41, 42: July 15, 16

We awoke to find the wind blowing fiercely out of the south. We still had not pounded in tent pegs, so our body weight was essential in holding the tent in place. Meaning we could not both leave at the same time. Jenny went into town for a shower and to launder clothing, to buy groceries and to find a couple of boxes, one of which was for mailing home Hermie.

To us, Hermie was a souvenir. We had deliberated the rights and wrongs of picking it up in the first place. Had we not, the next bounty hunter coming along would have. We disagreed with the senseless slaughter of these noble animals merely for their ivory. No doubt the hunters had their valid arguments. But to us, Hermie was just an old skull found on a desolate beach. Jenny had picked it up in the same spirit that she would have picked up a caribou antler or a snowy owl feather. Not for resale, but merely as a remembrance of our trip.

Next it was my turn for a shower. In the cold wind I found the walk into town exceptionally bracing. Point Lay, population 158, is part of the North Slope Borough, and seemed reasonably well funded with oil money perhaps. The town was nicely spread out, with gravel streets and street lamps. It even had bus service of all things. One bus made the rounds, without any passengers when I first saw it. But later I did notice one person climbing aboard. One could have walked across town in ten minutes, at least in summertime. In winter one might freeze in the same amount of time while waiting for the bus.

The washeteria-shower facility was well maintained and clean, and the showers and sauna were free of charge. The sauna would have felt nice, had it not been for my ongoing dehydration. The attendant was a friendly lady named Marie, and she asked me if I was one of the "crazy kayakers." Apparently Jenny had told her I was coming. Marie said she was born at the old village, across the lagoon.

I had not noticed any sled dog teams here in Pt. Lay, unlike the other villages we had visited. But I did see a few puppies running around loose, practically begging to be adopted. One followed me all the way across town and into the washeteria, but Marie promptly ordered it out.

I barely made it back to the tent before the onset of more rain. The storm intensified, and became a deluge that in the next 24 hours filled the open skiffs with several inches of water. With each gust the tent jumped around, and the sound of rain was a constant drumming. We spent the time resting and reading the same books we had already read cover to cover.

As the rain began to slacken, trucks and 4-wheelers started coming and going. Even a magnum-sized forklift began milling industriously about. Five men worked at dragging the fishing skiffs up and out of the rising water. Very few boats were pulled by the actual owners, it seemed. The big forklift became stuck in the mud, and two tractors were summoned to pull it free. The beach was small and we were sorry to be in the way of the heavy equipment. One of the tractor drivers came over to apologize for the equipment bothering us, and like every one here he was very friendly.

At least the rain was keeping most of the kids away, although we did surprise a teenage boy and girl snooping around. The guilty looks on their faces suggested that we had best keep an eye on things.

A lady named Lily Aniskett came by and invited us to pitch our tent in the lee of her house as a windbreak. Later her husband Charles stopped by with a load of salmon in the basket of his 4-wheeler. He offered us a couple and we gratefully accepted one. It was about 18 inches long. Someone else invited us up for tea, but we needed to hold down the tent.

At long last I went out and collected driftwood tent stakes, each about two feet long by one inch diameter. With the tent well secured, the storm almost seemed to go away. From the inside, the tent now stood still and

Charles Aniskett presenting us with a fresh-baked salmon still wrapped in aluminum foil.

quiet, despite the buffeting wind. This was a huge improvement, and I wondered that I had not staked it much sooner. Even then we could hardly relax because of the 4-wheelers and children – our fault for camping in such a busy and unlikely place. Jenny pan-fried the salmon for breakfast. It was delicious.

Later that evening, Jenny was just starting to cook dinner when Charles happened by again. "Hope you haven't cooked dinner yet," he said, handing her a baked salmon, fresh and piping hot from his wife's oven and nicely wrapped in foil. It, too, tasted superb.

Day 43: July 17

The wind was still blowing, but was down to about 15, and the lagoon was still white capped but nothing like before. We were eager to move on, so decided to give it a try.

We set off at 9:45 am carrying both 2½-gallon jugs and both half-gallon jugs of drinking water – enough to see us to the next village of Wainwright, some 90 miles north. The wind was angling slightly onto shore, and we figured the paddling would be easier on the lagoon's far side. So we struck a diagonal course northwest and paddled open water for an hour.

Wading through shallows, miles from land.

Approaching the far side, we encountered shoals, and these persisted most of the day. When the water became too shallow we turned back toward open water. When it deepened, we turned in toward shore. But rarely did we get closer than 1½-miles to shore. A few times it was more like twice that, especially after rounding the larger shoals and finding ourselves in what seemed like the middle of the ocean and paddling rough water. As much as we wanted to land and cook a hearty breakfast, and later, lunch, the shoals prevented it. Our greatest desire, however, was for northerly progress, so we stayed well out and kept churning the blades.

At long last, in the early afternoon we found a place where the water was fairly deep right up to the shore. We hauled out and cooked a quick lunch of leftover baked salmon and eggs. For once I did the cooking, seated on another whale vertebrae. As a matter of curiosity we checked the outside beach and found it clear of fresh animal tracks. High ground was in short supply. The entire sandbar was low lying, with nothing over seven feet.

We set off again, and now were able to paddle much closer in. The wind started veering from south through southwest, indicating approaching weather. Eventually we reached the lagoon entrance at Utukok Pass, and saw a tent cabin pitched on the south bank. If the locals camped on such low-lying ground, we figured the dangers of high surf or storm surge must be minimal. The lagoon entrance was half a mile wide, with a strong current running out, as indicated by a rip that extended bank-to-bank, and large surf festering the deeper water. In fact, even from a few miles back we had been hearing the distant roar of this surf.

Rounding the north bank, we came to a dead whale. At first we thought it was a small one, since its body was only 1½-feet out of the water. But as we drew near, we could see that most of the animal was submerged. How deep? I probed my paddle down and found no bottom. Yet the whale was not floating. It was resting on the bottom. This whale was huge! And it seemed strange to find it here in the lagoon.

The further we traveled the more the wind veered, west then northwest, and the darker the sky. The onset of this next front had manifested the day previously as an adumbration on the western horizon. Incredibly, after two gales back to back, it looked like we were in for a third. Fortunately, along this section we were able to paddle close to shore. Unfortunately, we now had stiff headwinds that continued veering, first through north and eventually north-northeast, at which point the wind rose to gale force.

The land was extremely low lying and devoid of vegetation. It looked more like a vast tidal flat, and offered no place for camping. We debated whether to turn back to the vicinity of the tent cabin. But far ahead were encouraging patches of higher ground. So we hunkered down and clawed ahead for another hour. Shoals appeared out in the lagoon, and we steered between them and the outlying bar, for their protection from the waves. I had not fitted my spray skirt and was now taking the occasional greenie into my cockpit, but nothing of any real danger.

Finally the wind became too much. We landed on the bar and started lining the boat, and thus traveled another quarter mile to the first area of higher, grass-covered ground and the first vegetation, really, since the pass. Here we found plenty of good camping.

So at 7:30 pm we pitched the tent in a light rain, and weighted it down internally with the water jugs, clothing bags, and so forth. Then we tied it to the yak and went searching for driftwood tent stakes. Not far from the tent we found a patch of downy feathers – goose or duck, possibly eider - and a whale vertebra for a bench. No recent animal tracks were in evidence, but a few bear tracks appeared to be three to four days old.

The evening was cold and so blustery that not a single mosquito was to be seen anywhere. The absence of these winged pests was so luxurious that we did not bother zipping the tent's netting doorway closed.

Days' Run: 30 n-mi, 10 hrs. Camp: 70° 07.500' N, 162° 28.166' W

Day 44: July 18

Ironically the wind calmed in the night, and we awoke to the sound of a few dozen mosquitoes buzzing around inside the tent. For some reason none seemed to have landed on us.

Setting out, we turned our backs to the lagoon and portaged the fifty yards across the sandbar. There we loaded the boat and embarked upon the open ocean, this at 9:00 am. The fog was thick, the air fairly still, and the pests followed in droves. For the initial hour we paddled in head nets, until one by one the winged adversaries dropped back. The morning was rather dark, and the fog cleared to reveal an equally leaden sky. To someone else the weather might have seemed dismal, but for us the conditions were perfect for making good progress and rounding the prominent headland of Icy Cape.

The coastline was low and sandy, and fairly unchanging. Finally the radio tower at Icy Cape hove into view, and at 2:00 pm we reached the cape itself. It was surprisingly low lying with a bit of a bar extending and no markers in evidence. The sea was somewhat agitated but nothing to cause concern. For the past several hours the wind had been light and from astern, but now was beginning to switch offshore. Within a quarter mile of the cape was an old, abandoned cabin.

A few miles farther along we landed and cooked a hearty breakfast of ground beef and eggs, followed by steaming cuppas. The wind was now blowing just hard enough to keep the mosquitoes at bay, at least as long as we kept our faces to the wind. The mosquitos clung in droves to our backs where they found protection from the wind.

We were always amazed to find seashells this far north. Here were large clams up to four and five inches, murex type snails, parts of crabs everywhere, sometimes starfish and sand crabs, occasional jellyfish, and even a bit of seaweed.

The wind began to increase, and a few miles beyond our cook site we noticed a dark object on shore far ahead. My first guess was a cabin, but Jenny noted that cabins do not normally move of their own volition. As we drew near we saw it was #22, a three or four year old patrolling the shore. It stopped and looked at us, then waded in excitedly chest deep. We had seen this behavior several times before, and figured the bear was mistaking us for some large aquatic creature drifting its way. Eventually the bear gave up and resumed wandering westward along the beach. The next time I turned around to look, it was running away, and this it continued for another five minutes until only a wee dot. The wind was blowing vigorously offshore and I could not imagine what had triggered the creature to flee, unless it had somehow caught a whiff of our cooking odors left behind on the beach. In any case we were encouraged by this type of reaction.

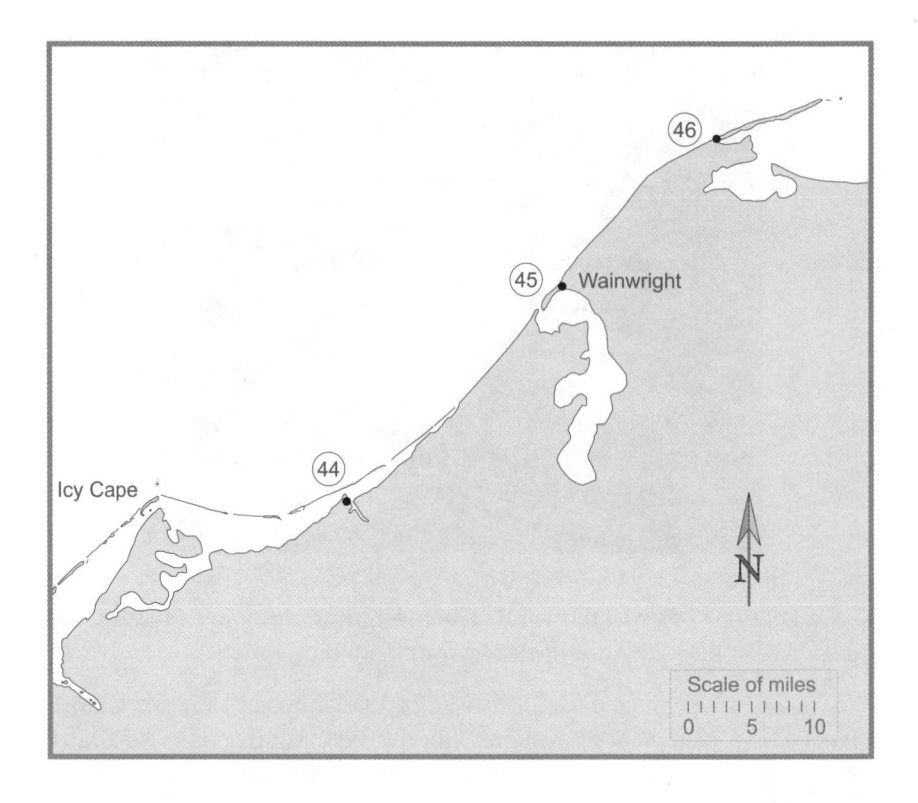

Mid afternoon the sun broke through, and for a while we paddled with suits unzipped. The wind began to veer, from south to west-northwest, and gradually built throughout the remainder of the day. Ultimately we found ourselves fairly flying along in a tail wind. The seas roughened and the ride became boisterous.

Before crossing Akoliakatut Pass we landed, and found some grass covered dunes that would have made nice camping. In these conditions the crossing of this pass would surely be frisky. We could not see land on the far side, nothing but a blank horizon save for a higher bluff farther along the coast. The map indicated it to be about one mile across. I was vaguely thinking of stopping for the day, but Jenny was eager to press on. So we set off and in fifteen minutes could see low-lying land ahead. Now in fairly heavy following seas we negotiated a line of breaking surf by keeping to its outside. Soon we were "running" parallel to shore, in wind fairly flinging us along. Often we had to stop paddling in order to maintain equilibrium in the bouncing and nearly breaking seas.

Ultimately, prudence called for us to get off the water. The sandbar was extremely low lying, so offered no possibility of camping. Behind it was the lagoon, which appeared less than a mile wide, as estimated by the sight of some higher cliffs on the mainland. We came to another pass, and figured we could simply duck into the lagoon and our troubles would be over. This did not prove so.

As we rounded the corner and entered the pass we found waves barreling out at about the same size as those barreling in. All were were about 2½-feet high, and the result was a washing machine effect that juddered bodies and nerves. Off to our right was a breaking rip, where water was leaping into the air. Landing on the backside of the bar was therefore out of the question. The high banks of the distant shore stood directly ahead of us. To our left was supposed to be the continuation of the lagoon spit, but we could see nothing of it. So we paddled into the lagoon and headed for the far shore.

The waves in the lagoon were much worse than those outside at sea, due to the current-induced wave interference. They were so rough that watching them tended to induce vertigo. I fixed my gaze on the distant shore and paddled by feel alone. And with Jenny also paddling resolutely, the yak proved its true worth. Laboring mightily into the tempest, we fairly clawed our way into the bay.

Eventually we neared shore and rounded a point of land, which turned out to be Nokotlek Point. Here we inadvertently scattered a huge brace of ducks and other waterfowl.

At 7:30 pm we ducked behind an elbow of land that protected a little bay so well that we coasted to shore in zero surf. This was a lovely little alcove with a flat and grassy area on which to camp, backed by low tundra hills. Caribou tracks were everywhere, along with their droppings. They obviously enjoyed grazing here. Also we found a wall tent site that looked like it had not been used in many years. We did not use it either, owing to the broadcast of trash. We spread our gear to dry, pitched the tent and secured it with many stakes – just in case - and reveled in the ambiance so remote, wild, and so fresh and peaceful. To think that we were above the 70th parallel in such a beautiful place. We felt privileged to be here.

Day's Run: 39 n-mi, 10½ hrs. Camp: 70° 19.585' N, 161° 00.773' W

Day 45: July 19

Rain fell hard in the night, and by morning we were feeling reluctant to rise and leave our cozy campsite, particularly as the wind was still blowing from the same direction, and the morning's temperature was quite low. But the prospects of making at least some distance along the inside shoreline prompted us into action. Looking out the tent's doorway we disturbed several dozen ducks and a handful of gulls enjoying the calm, protected waters of the little bay.

We set off at 8:00 am on a course diagonally across the bay, going directly downwind. We had expected a rough ride but found that even well into the bay the waves were less than 1½-feet. And with the wind at our backs we of course made great time. Fog shrouded the landscape, hiding even the outer sandbar. The morning was cold and grey, but we were pleased to be moving. And always the seabirds - on the water and in the air – lifted our spirits. Two or three times we came upon an adult with chicks. She would flog the water in the usual broken wing routine designed to distract us from her brood, while the little ones swam worriedly together in a tight-knit bundle. Sometimes with mother away in her broken wing act, other adults would come watch over the chicks and direct them which way to swim. We were sorry to distress these creatures, but were also encouraged at how they helped each other.

The mainland on our right was a succession of 30-foot bluffs interspersed with valleys. Tundra covered everything, right to the grassy shoreline. The lack of beach suggested a storm surge, and the ground was soaking wet from all the rain.

The map showed a long spit protruding into the lagoon adjacent its northernmost pass. Based on the previous day's experiences we decided to stay as far away from these passes as possible. We determined to portage the spit instead. But the portage proved unnecessary because the spit was submerged and only a few yards wide – again thanks to the storm surge. The hull scraped bottom only momentarily.

In another three or four miles we passed an exceptionally well-preserved ruin of an ancient sod dwelling. It had corner posts capped with horizontal beams all the way around in a rectangle, all standing on a sod mound. Surrounding the dwelling were stout driftwood stakes, weathered to a soft silvery-grey but still standing upright and holding firm. It was the best example of traditional Inupiat architecture we had seen thus far.

Tailwinds continued to push us favorably along, and eventually we reached the end of the lagoon. Here was a large creek flowing in, so into this we paddled, while still paralleling the outer seashore. The creek was shallow and for about half its length we had to pull the boat. It led into a sizeable lake, and this we paddled across. But reaching the far shore we could paddle no farther, at least in these protected waters. Cold rain was pummeling down and the wind was blowing a hefty 15 from the west and causing the surf to pound the outer seashore. Nearby on higher ground was a nice looking cabin. It looked lived in, although we could see no one.

We walked across the sandbar for a closer look at the surf. The seas were too rough, meaning that we would have to make camp and wait for the weather to subside. We returned to the lake and lugged the yak, without unloading it first, up to a place on the bar level enough for camping. But the ground here consisted of wet, fine-grained sand that made the prospects of pitching the tent anything but appealing. We had hoped to reach the village of Wainwright before its post office closed today at 6:00 pm. The time was now 2:00 pm. We returned to the seashore for a second look.

Standing there a long while, we studied the wave sets. The waves appeared to be about four feet high, and were breaking only sporadically but sometimes quite far out. Very occasionally there came a lull between sets, so we decided to attempt a break out.

Under the weight of the fully loaded kayak we again waddled like a couple of penguins. Putting the yak in position, we made everything ready and waited for just the right moment. Surf was not the only problem here. Also a large shore dump - caused by a long and hard backwash down the beach - was fairly omnipresent and unavoidable.

At the sight of a good lull approaching, we picked up the yak and waded into the sea. When Jenny was in to her knees, she set the bow down, but without paying attention to a large beach dump bearing down. The wave broke over the bow and washed back along the deck. Jenny's cockpit disappeared, then took on the appearance of flushing toilet. Quickly we labored the boat back up the beach, and bailed and sponged both cockpits.

Then came a second attempt, but not before I reminded Jenny to watch for the shore break this time, and to lift the bow high so that the wave would not inundate the deck. At the next right moment we ventured into the water. Jenny set the boat down knee deep. The next shore break poised, and Jenny lifted the bow. The break slid harmlessly beneath the kayak. She set the bow down and I gave the word. We both jumped aboard and started paddling furiously. Jenny was pumped with adrenaline and seemed to be paddling at least six times as hard as myself. Her blades reminded me of an electric eggbeater and I had never seen anyone paddle with such vigor. We fairly shot out across the water, leaping across wave after wave, spray flying mightily. Then suddenly we were out of harm's way and into relatively calm, at least non-breaking seas, free and clear.

Turning toward Wainwright we proceeded buoyantly on our way. The seas were rough, with waves to nearly five feet, but we were safe enough and with a quartering tailwind and a determined stroke, made very good time. The surf kept us far from shore, making us feel more like sea voyagers than coastal wanderers. Within 45 minutes we had warmed ourselves with exercise, and finally the rain ceased, allowing us to at least remove the sou'westers.

During the day we saw one dead walrus or seal, one live shearwater, some plovers, a few murres, and of coarse the usual loons and gulls. The area around the Kuk River (Wainwright Inlet) was rather shallow and breaking far out. But once around its corner we found a clear route all the way to the village. The highest waves were now only 3 to 4 feet, and we timed our exit well and sped to the beach, landing uneventfully at 4:20 pm.

I found an excellent tent site on a grass-covered, sandy knoll, 12 feet above sea level. To this we carried a few of the heavier things, then the yak. Jenny grabbed her "grab it and run to the post office bag," which she had prepared at our previous camp. With that she headed along the beach for the town standing about a quarter mile in the distance. I began pitching the tent and establishing camp. The reason we tended to stop this far from the villages was for the peace and quiet. But soon a 4-wheeler came growling along. The fellow pulled to a stop and asked where we had come from. But when I said Shishmaref he sort of laughed beneath his breath, as though my reply was obviously meant as a joke. He asked whether we had been to Point Lay, and I said yes, and named off some of the other villages we had visited. He asked if I needed any help, then left me to my camp chores.

After pitching the tent I placed some of the drier things inside to hold it down, then set about placing our sodden gear out to dry - mittens, hats, life jackets, and so forth. I had failed to seal the chart case properly, so the charts were soaked. Also I found water in the aft hatch, leading me to suspect that its bulkhead was leaking slightly.

I was just finishing when Jenny returned. Our resupply box had arrived, and there at the post office she pulled the needed things out and mailed the remainder home. We crawled into the tent, prepared our laundry, and Jenny generously set off for town a second time. This left me with little clothing, and I soon realized just how cold the day was. Sleeping quilt to the rescue.

Jenny returned freshly showered. The laundry facility had closed for the day, but the grocery store was still open, and also she had filled our water jug. The wind had piped up and the sea was now tumultuous. It almost seemed like a miracle that we had traveled the thirty miles today.

The postmaster, Kenny, whom Jenny had telephoned from Point Lay, had expressed surprise that we had paddled the distance in only three days. He asked if we had seen any animals, to which Jenny replied yes, one grizzly. He wanted to know if it was a big and aggressive one. Jenny affirmed it was, and he thought it might have been the same ornery character that had been raiding the out-lying cabins, including his own. This bear, he said, had broken into his place by pushing in a window, frame and all. Once inside it wreaked all sorts of havoc, including pulling a hanging lantern and the hook on which it hung from the ceiling. Kenny later found the lantern a few hundred yards across the tundra. While Jenny was at the post office several villagers came and went, and Kenny told them about "the kayakers." According to Jenny, the villagers had responded with much interest. The Search & Rescue people also seemed concerned about our journey, and later we learned that a walrus hunter had drowned the previous week in a strong blow that hurled 12-foot waves onto the beach.

Hotel rooms went for a whopping $175 a night, so we passed on that. The hotel's restaurant had also closed for the evening, so Jenny was not able to bring back hot food. But the owner had kindly invited us back for lunch the following day. And while in the lobby Jenny was quick to notice a used book exchange.

At the Co-op store she met a friendly clerk named Abbey Ungudruk, (g and d not pronounced). When Abbey heard that we had come from Point Lay, she asked Jenny if we had met Lily and Charles Aniskett. Lily was her cousin. Abbey emphasized the fact that Charles was Indian, not Eskimo. From the store's pay phone Jenny called Lily and Charles back at Point Lay. They had kindly asked us to get in touch once we arrived at Wainwright, to let them know we were safe. Jenny thanked them again for the delicious salmon.

Back at camp, we were just settling in when the first torrent of children rushed in. "Anyone in there?" they asked a couple of times. Jenny stuck her head out, and in a stern voice demanded, "What do you want?" That was enough to send them packing. This was entirely uncharacteristic of my easy-going mate, but then who was I to complain? All I wanted was a little peace and quiet.

Day's Run: 30 n-mi, 8 hrs. Camp: 70° 38.5' N, 160° 02.00' W

Day 46: July 20

The morning was blustery and the seas were even more boisterous than when we had landed. So we decided on a rest day, if such a thing was possible so close to a village. Fortunately the store was well stocked, and Jenny had bought steaks, fresh fruits and vegetables. Before we could cook, I needed to clean the stove, the first time of the trip.

Even with a separate cleaning needle, this type of jet was difficult to clean. The needle, when inserted top to bottom, only poked the debris and sludge into the nipple's interior. This I tried to clean with a whittled stick. But every time I reassembled the stove and primed it, the pressure shoved the debris back into the jet and re-clogged it. The shaker needle had no effect. We needed some kind of cleaning tool that forced the debris out the top where it could be wiped away. Later I contrived just such a tool, but for now were using a stove that burned only half-heartedly.

We spent the day resting, eating, napping, reading, and dealing with occasional villagers. I did not go into town, not even for a shower, because I did not feel our gear was safe from the children. They meant no harm, but their curiosity was insatiable.

Bang! Someone fired a rifle at the tent. I leapt outside just in time to see four youths on two motorbikes speeding away. I chased after them a ways but could not match their speed. Returning to the tent I discovered they had only thrown a rock. By chance it had impacted where Jenny's head was. Fortunately, between rock and head was a thick paperback novel, and this had taken the brunt of the blow.

The next batch of youths introduced themselves very congenially. We were still fairly fuming but did not let it show. These kids were quite nice, and interested in the kayak.

The wind and seas had calmed, and we realized that peace and quiet were not to be. We decided to depart. As we were packing bags inside the

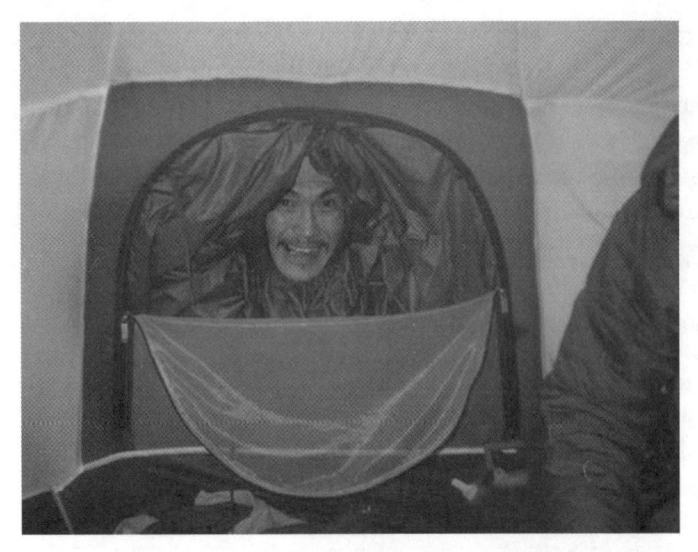

"No heater in there!? Come on over to my house and warm up. I've got coffee and hot chocolate."

tent, yet another 4-wheeler pulled up. We had abandoned the notion of trying to entertain everyone, and by now were trying instead to ignore them. A voice spoke up: "Anyone in there?" It sounded like another kid. I gave a polite "yes" and went about my business. A man's face appeared, pressed against the mosquito netting and perfectly framed by the ventilating hole we had left in the tunnel. The face was carved in the typical weather-toughened Inupiaq visage, and rounded by a fur trimmed parka hood. The expression was that of curiosity and friendliness. "Getting ready to go to sleep?" We felt like miniature figures in a museum diorama, and this struck me as uproariously funny. Always the Inupiaq were intrigued by the idea of camping in such a small tent. "No heater in there!? Come on over to my house and warm up. I've got coffee and hot chocolate."

Danny stationed himself there for some time, while we continued packing. Eventually I stepped out and found his wife standing there also.

A young lad was hanging around, throwing rocks at things. He would not tell us his name, and we wondered if he might have been our culprit. He was a nice kid, not in the least malicious, and he pointed out a couple of whales swimming past the village several hundred yards offshore. Danny had told us to watch for grey whales. "We don't hunt them because they don't taste good." To keep the kid's busy little hands occupied, we asked him to help carry some gear down to the water's edge – under close supervision.

I paddled along shore while Jenny walked into town with mail to send and trash to dispose of. Daisy and Harry drove by, each on separate 4-wheelers, and Daisy gave Jenny a lift on the back of her vehicle. Harry bantered that if I forgot to stop for her, he and Daisy would drive her out to Point Franklin and would race me there.

Daisy and Harry had stopped by our camp earlier today, and we had enjoyed an interesting chat. They were both in their late 40's and had lived in Wainwright all their lives, except that Harry had been to Oregon for schooling at some sort of ex-military camp. Daisy worked as an Inupiat language teacher's aid at the school. Harry seemed to know a lot about North Slope Borough history. He said the people had moved out of Icy Cape in the early 20's, that the old village of Point Lay was abandoned in the late 50's, and in both cases people dispersed to other villages.

Harry had several relatives in Point Lay. He said the people there were "laid back." We told him about the storm, and that we had camped by all the boats and how the people had not seemed to care much for their boats. He laughed and said, "Yeah, they sit around smoking dope all the time and laugh when their boats have problems." Harry wore a permanent smile on his face and radiated happiness. He said he encouraged his kids to move to Fairbanks or Anchorage. But apparently they were not interested because of the dreadful stories they saw on the daily news.

Harry explained that there were hundreds of old sod houses - like the ones we had seen – in this area. The people had made them by standing driftwood on end for the walls, piling sod against that for insulation, then building the ceiling in much the same way. The entrance was a hole dug into the ground, tunneled under the wall, and up through the floor. He once found one of these dwellings landscaped with a pair of whale skulls, one on each side of the entrance, and with whale bones standing upright around the house for dramatic effect.

I asked about the dredging project visible in the foreground. The crews had been dredging sand from the seabed and pumping it onto the beach via two-foot diameter steel pipes. The intent was apparently to curtail beach erosion. Harry laughed and said that they had caused the erosion to begin with, by stripping the beach of gravel for making the airstrip. The newly placed sand seemed to be eroding away.

Harry said the weather was much rainier than normal, and that the pack ice was now 30 miles offshore, as measured by people who had gone out with a GPS. He never took his own boat out without first calling Barrow Weather, because the storms could come up so quickly. One could even drive a truck to Barrow during low tide, he said. He had killed only one polar bear in his life. The bear had followed him all the way home, right into the village, where it posed a serious danger to everyone. He had seen many polar bears in winter while hunting seals and walrus. When he found bears with a fresh killed walrus, he chased them away temporarily and took the ivory, then let the bears return to the feed.

Harry explained how they kept warm during the winter, by eating meat: seal, walrus and whale. Even frozen meat would keep you warm, he said. He described how they rendered the fat then preserved the meat in the oil. When they went out on their snowmobiles in winter, they took chunks of this frozen meat and fat to eat for warmth.

I mentioned to Harry that we had seen what looked like a very small, dead walrus floating in the water. Harry explained that the walrus hunters would sometimes shoot both mother and baby; otherwise the baby would start squawking and the other walrus would come to its aid, and so endanger the hunters.

Wainright residents gathered on the beach to see us off. Danny is the tall one; to his right, Harry and Daisy.

I arrived at the beach where Jenny, Harry, and Daisy were waiting, in the company of a few other villagers including Danny. Coming ashore, I caught a small wave and surfed to the beach in a most sprightly fashion. Jenny grabbed the bow and pulled the yak out of the water. For once we looked like we knew what we were doing - until Daisy pointed out several inches of water sloshing in my cockpit. Earlier during breakout I had caught a small wave, but had forgotten to bail. At least this spoke well of the drysuits.

Everyone showed interest in the kayak, especially after we told them we had made it ourselves. They scrutinized it along with our gear. In particular they admired our mukluks for their lightness of weight. Jenny explained that we had made them from a pattern sent to us from a native friend at Point Hope. With fond farewells we cast off just after midnight, actually 12:30 am July 21.

Day 47: July 21

The sky was darkly clouded, and the wind blowing only 5 to 8 knots fine on the starboard bow so the seas were rather flat. We followed coastal bluffs several miles, noting unfortunately the trash in many of the ravines. In the Arctic regions, the landfill - as we know it in the lower 48 - is not feasible because the permafrost prevents digging. Instead, the villages tend to use incinerating areas, although inevitably some of the trash would escape when the wind blew strongly.

All along the way, the air reeked of whales' breath. And indeed, far offshore we could see plumes of a large pod of grey whales. The villagers had said they had seen belugas just offshore the day of our arrival. Hunters had gone in pursuit, but the seas had roughened and concealed them. They also said they had seen killer whales.

Point Belcher was a long, low coastal pan backed by a couple of lagoons. Here we encountered an increasing northerly that raised a gnarly chop and taxed our arms. This went on for five miles until easing and allowing easier passage.

Passing the abandoned village of Atanik, I stepped out and climbed the dunes for a look around, searching for the best place to portage into Peard Bay. In the vicinity were quite a few old sod dwellings in various stages of decay. The bay started just here, but was several hundred yards inland so I returned to the boat and we paddled another half mile.

In 1871 the entire whaling fleet was driven ashore here by pack ice. More than thirty ships were crushed, and even after all these years quite a few timbers and other debris lay strewn about. The pieces were extremely weathered and most lay at least partially buried in the sand.

At 6:30 am we portaged our outfit a few hundred yards across a low-lying sandbar. Initially we were very chilled, but the exercise soon warmed us, and by the time we started pitching the tent, we no longer needed our gloves. This was good because pitching the coliseum required a certain amount of dexterity.

July 21, 6 hrs, morning stop: 70°, 50.896' N, 159° 20.008' W

July 21 continued

After a lengthy stint of rain we rose and finished portaging the 50 yards to the lagoon, which here was an extension of Peard Bay. The clouds were breaking apart and an icy wind was bowling stiffly from the northwest.

A few plovers were foraging in the shallows nearby. They were so energetic and cheery, and did not seem bothered by our readying the kayak for departure.

We set off at 3:00 pm, still July 21, and paddled to a batch of shoals delineating the lagoon's far shore. We stepped out and dragged the boat over the shoals and into Peard Bay proper, then with a strong tailwind shoving us along, we plied the protected waters, unable to see for any real distance through the thickening fog.

Nearing Asiniak Point the shoreline swung northwest, and this placed the wind and seas on our beam and forced us into overdrive mode to prevent being driven ashore. Across the way, on the Point Franklin sandbar was what appeared to be a small tent city - presumably the group of archeologists at Pingasagruk, spoken of in the village. Twice their support helicopter buzzed overhead in the fog.

Reaching the point, we rounded the corner and once again benefited from a strong tailwind in protected waters, at least for a couple of miles. Beyond that lay the open mouth of Kuarua Bay. We debated the rationality of

150 -- *Siku Kayak*

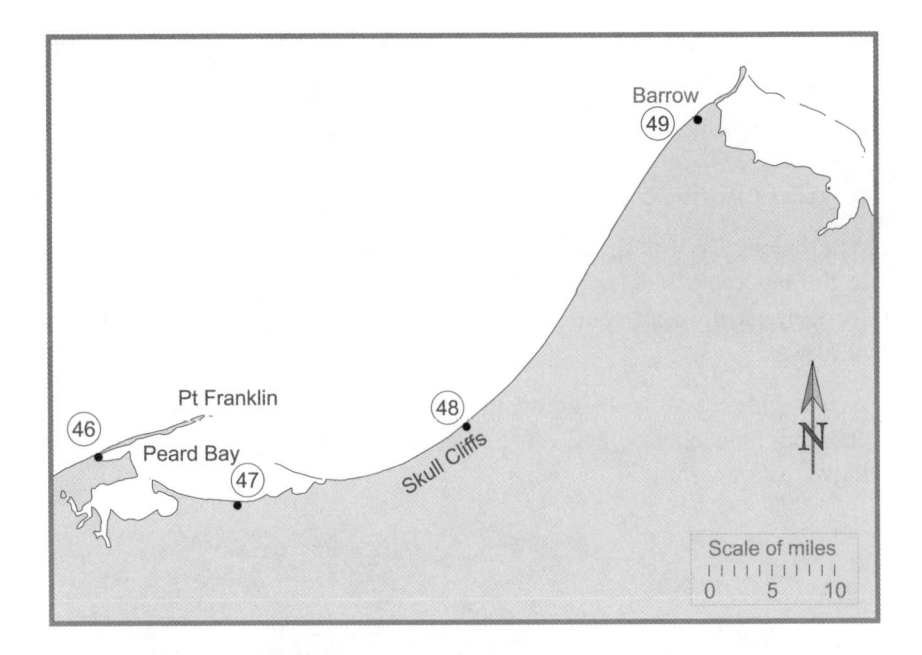

making the 1½-mile required jump, rather than calling it quits for the day and retiring into the sanctuary of the coliseum to let the gale simply blow itself out. But ever eager for more mileage we pressed ahead.

We were half way across when the wind increased to 30 knots and the seas began tossing the yak around like the proverbial cork. This was nerve wracking, nevertheless we continued toward Eluksingiak Point, unable to see it specifically although we could at least make out a long stretch of mud cliffs. Toward these we steered for what appeared to be the nearest land.

Reaching shore at long last, we landed at the cliff's left edge and dragged the boat out of the thrashing water and onto the grass. Here the lay of the land was most perplexing. A long spit extended far to our left, and we wondered whether we might have mistakenly paddled back out to Franklin Point. I should not have gone slack on my compass navigation, because visuals alone can be misleading.

Bracing ourselves in the icy blast we spread the maps in the kayak's scant lee, and plotted a GPS position fix. Fortunately this indicated that we had come the correct way. So we dragged the kayak into a nearby lake, and after struggling through knee-deep quicksand-like mud a ways to deeper water, paddled to the lake's far shore then dragged another 20 feet ahead into the bay. Now in large waves and 20 knot quartering tailwinds we proceeded ahead. Twice I took combers into my cockpit, and these reminded me not to become lax also with the spray skirt. I sponged the bilge and fitted the skirt.

All along here the shore showed evidence of the sea's rising as much as three feet. Again, this was not tidal, but storm surge.

After skirting a long line of mud cliffs, at 7:00 pm we pulled into the mouth of a creek, and dragged the boat over a shoal granting access to a pretty little lake. On its pristine shore we hauled out and pitched the tent.

A hundred feet away we sat, backs to the frigid wind, and enjoyed a few shafts of sunshine while cooking a reviving pot of corn spaghetti.

Each of our campsites along this coast had been unique, and this one had its own wild and vibrant feel, with heavy, bulbous clouds speeding overhead, the sting of wind off ice, sudden fingers of sunlight sparkling then gone, tiny wavelets on our private lake trying to mimic the rougher waves out at sea – all amid a lovely carpet of green grass and tundra. Caribou paths led to the lake and beyond, and the caribou's fresh tracks were imprinted in the soft sand and mud at the shoreline. A more exquisite setting would have been hard to find.

Day's Run: 35 n-mi, 10 hrs. Camp: 70° 47.355' N, 158° 46.457' W

Day 48: July 22

The morning was cold, grey and foggy when we shoved off at 8:30 am. In light snow flurries and light headwinds we proceeded along the bay.

Reaching its end, we found an inlet leading to a small lake. On the shores of this lake we met a group of walrus hunters and their three-man Korean tv crew. Everyone appeared friendly, so we landed ashore for a chat. At first they spoke to us in a foreign tongue. Not knowing quite what to say, I asked, "Japanese?" to which they replied, "No, we're from Barrow." After that they spoke English. To us they did not look Inupiaq, partly white perhaps, with some oriental thrown into the mix. They had recently killed two walrus, a female and a very large male, and showed us the tusks with heads still attached. They explained that they would boil the heads until the skulls turned snow white, for easier removal of the flesh. The tusks were worth about $2,000 per set, the fellow said. They also had gunnysacks of the meat. When asked what they did with that, they said "Same thing you do with cows." Perhaps, but we wondered if it would more likely find its way to the sled dogs.

Saying goodbyes we paddled to the lake's far end, then carried the fully laden boat in 30 yard bits across the bar to the shore. A few miles of paddling and we reached a fish camp, and were grinding slowly past in strong headwinds when a woman came out of a wall tent and very kindly invited us in for coffee. No doubt the walrus hunters were based here, and had radioed word of our arrival. But the surf prevented an easy landing, so we waved our thanks and kept going.

The tidal range along northern Alaska is less than six inches, but a strong westerly wind can raise the sea several feet. For this reason we never camped on a low sand bar lacking access to higher ground. The highest sea-rise in our experience was about three feet, shown above. For half a day the beaches and lower sand bars were submerged. Contrast the same type of beach, photo below, a few days later.

The headwinds became so strong that in another half mile we had to land anyway. And Jenny started lining the boat.

Rounding a corner we encountered - of all things - boulders blocking the way. Towing the yak and me faithfully onward, Jenny climbed over and around until reaching an impasse. I disconnected the towline and advised

her to scale the bluffs and parallel the shore to a beach visible ahead. Now the going was particularly slow, with me paddling solo and the wind still blowing strongly out of the northeast.

Eventually I reached the rendezvous but could not draw too close because of the surf. Jenny threw me the line, but without taking the trouble to untangle it first. On her second attempt she threw her tangles only a short ways further. I waited, but when she started to tie what looked like a rock to the line, presumably for better heaving, I figured that in the interests of safety - my own - I had better move out of firing range.

For the next couple of hours I slogged ahead, while Jenny merely sauntered along the beach. Nowhere could we find an easy landing.

Suddenly a blast of wind slammed me in the back and sent me and the kayak reeling. How could such a thing happen, I wondered, while paddling stiff headwinds? I hadn't a clue. Then the wind died, and started blowing east. This was still a strong headwind, but was perfect for lining because it knocked back the waves.

I landed, and Jenny cooked a pot of macaroni and cheese, and reviving cuppas. Then bundled to the max I sat in my cockpit steering while Jenny once again pulled. I grew extremely chilled and occasionally held my double mitted hands in front of my face to help check the wind. A few miles farther we switched roles, then reaching a suitable landing at 7:00 pm we decided to make camp on a three-foot rise overlooking a creek and lake.

After pitching the coliseum and securing our gear, we explored the immediate area, as was our usual practice in the absence of rain. Whenever out walking we were careful to scan the horizons both inland and seaward. No surprises. Lying on the tundra not far from camp was an old, discarded trappers sled. On a distant hill stood a lone caribou - head down and grazing, then head up and watching, then head down and grazing again. Fresh tracks were everywhere, all caribou, none bear. We retired into the coliseum and slept well.

Day's Run: 20 n-mi, 10½ hrs. Camp: 70° 52.434' N, 157° 46.464' W

Day 49: July 23 – Reaching the top of Alaska

Setting off at 8:30 am into light tailwinds, we paddled buoyantly along. The mud bluffs extended for quite some distance along the coast, in fact practically the entire way to the town of Barrow.

Seeing a young caribou wandering along shore, we steered toward it. As we came close it stepped mistrustfully away.

Paddling along the Skull Cliffs.

By midday the tailwinds had increased, but for some reason the seas were not growing much over two feet, so we enjoyed the boost. The south wind was extraordinarily warm and made for the first balmy day in weeks.

Squatting on the western horizon was a band of gleaming white - undoubtedly the pack ice. Very recently it had obviously been hard ashore, as evidenced by the brash and blocks adrift and aground.

Rounding the final bend we raised the sight of Barrow, and at 5:00 pm landed behind a small cluster of buildings. The day had been long and tiring, and our equilibrium was a bit off keel, for as we lugged the boat ashore Jenny tripped and crashed into a heap. In the process she bent her eyeglasses and scratched a finger. She simply picked herself back up, finished the carry, and after shedding drysuit she set off blithely to find the post office, leaving me to watch the boat. One of my jobs was to dig out the miniature pliers and straighten her glasses.

She returned lugging a heavy resupply box - one of two we had mailed. I daubed her finger with antiseptic, then she returned for the second box. We had been promising each other a motel room once we reached the top of Alaska, but Jenny had learned that the closest one was fully booked – and anyway it went for an excessive $180 per night. The only other motel was run down, with questionable characters hanging about. It went for $120 and had no safe place for the yak.

We set up camp next to a small building on skids. The yak and tent fit nicely between that and a large skiff. The impromptu campsite was well protected and hidden, yet handy to town - even despite the larger buildings and compact gravel. Jenny made one more trip for a pizza and a few

Camped semi-hidden between a couple of small buildings

groceries. Then at last we were free to enjoy ourselves with a hot meal and secure shelter.

After dinner Jenny sorted our food for the next leg while I wrote in the journal. Showers were available at the Community Gym, and were open until 11:00 pm, so she went for a shower while I remained at camp to keep an eye on things.

The people here seemed more aloof than the villagers away to the south and west. But at least they left us alone, and this allowed us the rest we needed.

Day's Run: 34 n-mi, 8½ hrs. Camp: 71° 17.556' N, 156° 47.335' W

Day 50: July 24 - Barrow

Rising early, I walked across town 15 minutes to the gym. The manager said we had been lucky with the ice, because it had blown offshore only two days earlier. Normally, he said, it did not move away until the first or second week of August.

After the shower I returned to camp, and Jenny went off to mail a few post cards and a box of unneeded gear. On the way back she bought groceries and placed a few phone calls. And finally she filled our water bottle at the town's water works.

We broke camp and carried the empty yak back down to water's edge. Into it we loaded three weeks worth of food and six gallons of water. I broke out through the small surf and paddled along the coast, while Jenny walked along shore to the gas station at the far north end of town. There she filled our stove's fuel bottle for a mere 49 cents. At least something here was cheap.

A long and narrow sand spit extends several miles north from Barrow, and rather than paddle all the way round it, we figured we could more easily portage. So Jenny continued walking along the road, looking for the best place.

The portage was several hundred yards long, but with considerable tugging we managed to drag the loaded yak over the grassy tundra, rather than carry it.

The wind was still 15 to 20 from the southwest, so was on the starboard beam as we paddled across the inlet. In such conditions we realized the futility of rounding Brant Point, so we hauled ashore in the lee and stepped onto the tundra, which here was only three feet above sea level. Ironically, after we had settled into the tent, the wind died. But we were tired and figured we could use the extra rest. We only hoped that the wind would not start blowing strongly from the north, because any waves over three feet high might reach camp.

Day's Run: 6 n-mi, 3 hrs. Camp: 71° 20.107' N, 156° 34.996' W

From Shishmaref we had paddled 790 miles of Bering and Chukchi Sea coastline to Barrow. Beyond was another 425 miles of Beaufort Sea coastline to the next village of Kaktovik

Day 51: July 25

Rain fell during the night, and the morning's wind was a mere 5-knot puff from the northeast. We set off at 6:30 am and paddled around Brant Point. Just south of the point we saw an intricate fish trap serviced by an inflatable dinghy parked on the tundra.

As we rounded the point we met stiff headwinds coming from the southeast. These would stay with us the entire day. And in fact, the day was to be one of the more strenuous of the trip thus far. To minimize fetch we hugged the shore most of the way, and because of this we went many extra miles.

Barrow sits at the most northerly tip of Alaska, and from there the coast tends east and very gradually south. And this coast was like nothing we had seen. The tundra met the sea in an abrupt step, one to ten feet in height. The tundra and its underlying peat averaged about eight inches thick, and below that was permafrost, or in many places pure ice. How ironic to see pretty flowers growing on an eight-inch pad of tundra sitting on eight feet of ice. Nature has its wondrous ways. The sea was melting this ice and undermining it, and large blocks had tumbled onto their sides, taking their green bonnets with them.

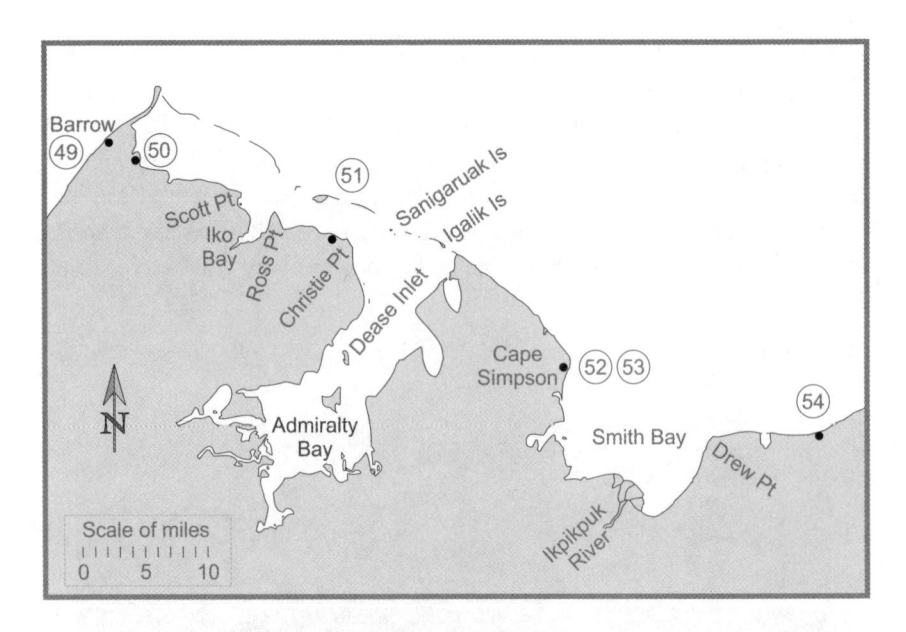

The day was warm, as Arctic climes go, maybe in the low 50's, and the exposed ice and permafrost were melting, sending large chunks of soil and peat sloughing into the sea. The churning surf was grinding the humus into fine particles and sending them along their way, to become future shoals perhaps. Four young caribou stood atop one ten-foot permafrost block, watching us pass. One seemed curious and allowed us to come fairly close before it ambled away. A brown fox with a luxuriously thick fur coat did much the same. It seemed to be young but we could not tell

Few had paddled this stretch in modern times, so we knew very little about it

for sure. And of course we saw quite a few birds, including a young gull with a broken wing. We saw neither people nor camps.

We paddled into Iko Bay a ways, then with wind and seas on the beam we pointed the bow towards the far shore. This crossing seemed a bit uncertain at first, because land at the far side was hardly visible. But in fact the bay was only a couple of miles wide.

At 4:30 pm we stopped for the day, just short of Christie Point on what appeared to be the last piece of high ground, which was all of about three feet above sea level. The wind served us well at this camp, keeping the bugs away and drying our clothing and gear. Bear signs were absent, and because the stiff wind was blowing offshore, we figured we could cook in reasonable safety. So we set up a cooking station 100 yards from camp, and Jenny prepared cuppas and a nice spaghetti with meat. Looking through the monocular across Elson Lagoon to the north, we could see

Cooper Island as a long, low sandbar, and just beyond that, the glimmering polar pack.

Day's Run: 25 n-mi, 10 hrs. Camp: 71° 10.704' N, 155° 38.191' W

Day 52: July 26

Beneath an overcast sky we set off at 7:00 am into a light easterly breeze. The projection that is Christie Point had silted-in to its west, and this required paddling around a cluster of sandbars. Reaching the immense Dease Inlet, we headed west-northwest into open seas on a course bound for Sanigaruak Island. This island was only four miles away, but was not visible. So part way across I activated Geepus to check our position, and again about an hour later because we still could not see the island - due largely to mirages, as it turned out. Mirages affect sea kayakers in particular because we sit so close to the water. This vantage makes the mirrages all the more pronounced. Ironically they tend to raise the background and obscure the foreground – which in this case was our intended island.

Reaching the island at last, we paddled through a rip, then a strong tidal current flowing into Dease Inlet. Once around the island we landed on its backside. The highest point of land here was a scant two feet. Bits of driftwood lay strewn about, so apparently the seas did not inundate the place very often. The next island in the chain was again not visible, so

Across the top of Alaska we often paddled out of sight of land.

this time I plotted a few waypoints on the chart and keyed them into the magic box.

The wind-driven salt spray coated our eyeglasses continually, and made them difficult to see through. We could have used miniature windshield wipers. Lacking these, we fashioned a couple of squeegees from the plastic lid of a potato chips can. These worked great, even without a fresh water rinse.

The southern sky was turning coal black as we set off for yet another unseen island, and while moving past our final point of land we sensed a strong counter current. A south wind piped up, and from that direction the sky was beginning to look like a solid wall of blackness.

Finally catching sight of the next island, we paddled quite hard but seemed to be making scant progress. Anyway, this island looked more like a sandbank - not sufficient for protection in a storm. The sky looked like an imminent nightmare, and we needed to get off the water. I figured that if we turned around, the current would sweep us quickly back to our previous island. Jenny thought the island ahead looked small only because it was still in the distance. I should have listened, but instead turned around. We paddled full tilt on a reciprocal heading toward our original island, which had long since dipped below the horizon, and so went for 30 or 40 minutes until Jenny noticed a low-lying island off to our right. The current had been sweeping us south. We swung right and steered for our island, and finally landed at our previous place in its lee.

For some reason the tempest held off, so we walked around to keep warm while waiting to see what the weather would do. The blast never did hit. False alarm. The horribly black sky had been nothing but an innocuous rain shower, and most of it had missed us.

We set off again, 1½ hours after we had the first time, and before long could see the next island once again on the distant horizon. But this time the sun came out and we enjoyed a most leisurely jaunt. Welcome to the Arctic, land of contrasts.

Despite its first appearance, this island – called Igalik - turned out to be far larger than the previous one, and would have provided vastly better shelter. It even had a barge grounded on its higher dune, and this might have served as a good windbreak.

Along the shore of Igalik Island we paddled a considerable distance. Then leaving it behind we again traversed open water to the next island, now in light headwinds. And so the process repeated itself throughout the afternoon, first paddling a long, low island, then crossing open water to the barely discernable next island. The pack ice was visible about a mile to the north, and a few floes were much closer.

Bucking stiff headwinds for a while, we landed, and I lined the boat while Jenny steered. The water was crystal clear and painfully cold if you put your hand into it. Notable on this beach were dead jellyfish of all sizes, a good supply of driftwood, and tracks of caribou - which seemed odd because the nearest real land was miles away across Fatigue Bay.

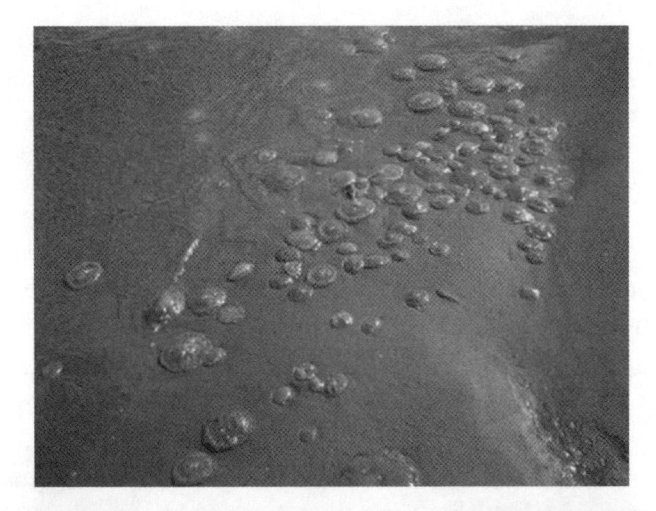

From my slightly higher vantage I could see a large herd of caribou on that far shore - perhaps 200 or 300 animals. Later during my jaunt we happened upon a lone caribou. It stopped and pondered us awhile, then galloped away. Either the sea between this island and the mainland was very shallow, or the caribou had made a remarkably long swim.

Jenny lined for a while, then together we paddled in heavy rain as another black cloud passed overhead. A north wind began wafting us along, and as we reeled away the miles this wind gathered strength. We passed a group of buildings that looked like a long abandoned military or scientific base. The former occupants had left the coast littered in rusting oil drums.

Farther along, the shore comprised higher bluffs of permafrost, and near Cape Simpson these bluffs reached skywards sometimes 20 or 30 feet. We planned to haul out just beyond the cape, but found a fish camp comprising a cabin, 4-wheeler and other signs of habitation, so we continued another third of a mile just past the Ikpikpuk River, and at 5:30 pm pulled in behind a protecting spit. Its protection was so good that instead of the three-foot breaking seas, we landed on a calm shore. The tundra here was only about four feet above the sea, but offered excellent camping.

When pitching the coliseum in strong wind such as this, we usually started by positioning the kayak directly upwind, and with its beam facing our prospective site. Two lines led from the deck, down the side of the boat opposite us, and under the hull. These lines then served as ground-level anchor points, to which we attached the tent prior to pitching it. This prevented the wind from blowing the tent away mid-pitch.

With Jenny at one end of the tent and me at the other, we would then feed the long poles through the equally long fabric sleeves. Numb fingers and blasts of cold wind did not assist this process, and trying to rush was a good way to tear something. Which is how we managed to rip another small hole in a sleeve today. But it was easily mended with a bit of duct tape.

Once the coliseum was pitched, we loaded our gear into it to help hold it down, then pounded stakes all around. For stakes we normally scrounged pieces of driftwood because they were far stronger than the small aluminum ones included with the tent. The result was as storm-proof a shelter as one could expect from seven poles and a bag of nylon.

Day's Run: 29 n-mi, 10½ hrs (not counting backtrack). Camp: 70° 59.710' N, 154° 34.614' W

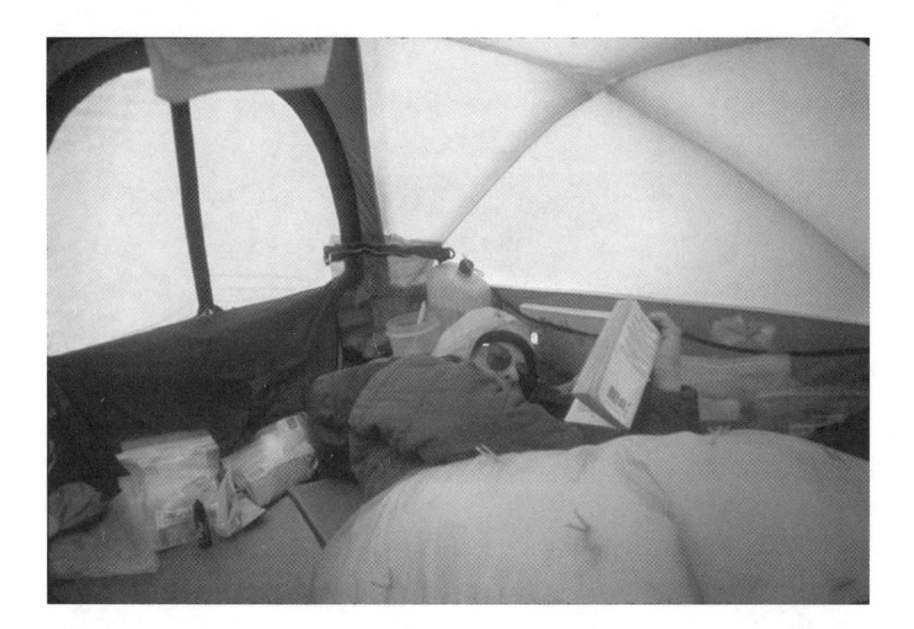

Day 53: July 27 - Stormbound

The morning was grey and frigid, with a strong wind blowing west-northwest - directly offshore. Normally this would have been fine, but not while trying to round the offlying shoals visible in the distance. So we bundled in all our warm clothing and ventured out to explore the surroundings. The ground was littered with droppings of caribou and geese, and on the beach were fresh tracks of fox. A while later, two boats came from across the bay into the stiff wind and chop, and landed at the cabin at Cape Simpson, but did not stay long.

The shoreline below our camp was well protected behind a four-foot bluff, and here little plovers and sandpipers were busy plucking small delicacies at the waterline. Taking the clue, Jenny climbed down the bank with stove and cookpot in hand, and found a clod of tundra that had tumbled down the bank and managed to land grassy side up. Seated comfortably on this tundra stool, she proceeded to cook a meal. The small birds ventured to within a couple feet, almost as though checking what was on the menu.

We spent the day in the tent, sleeping and reading. The weather became so severe that we went outside only when necessary, although once for some leg exercise I wandered inland a quarter mile to a lake. Mid afternoon the wind strengthened further, and became laced intermittently with rain.

Day 54: July 28 – Smith Bay

By early morning the wind had diminished, so despite the chill we set off at 5:00 am in an eight-knot tailwind, hoping to cross Smith Bay directly to Drew Point, an ambitious fifteen miles distant. But before we had managed only half a mile the wind increased to 12 knots and swung around to the south, putting itself broad on our starboard bow and raising a lumpy sea. This did not portend a safe transit, so we stood back for shore and resigned ourselves to paddling around this huge bay.

The next five miles of coast southwards were fronted with the occasional offlying shoal, and one of these necessitated our dragging and push-carting the boat - sitting on the deck while pushing with one leg - a few hundred yards to open water.

Still heading south, we jumped a two-mile gap where the land ahead was not visible. Now in the Piasuk River delta, we kept well off, one to two miles, to avoid its shoals.

Paddling south another three or four miles we reached the main Ikpikpuk River delta, spanning the next twelve miles of coast. We stayed well out, but even then encountered shallows that required us to steer even further out. Occasionally the shallows were indicated from a distance by large, driftwood logs grounded on the shoals. Still, it was an eerie sensation to be paddling in only a foot of water far from the sight of any land, and knowing that the next possibility of a landing was many miles ahead. This was not the place for making mistakes.

Eventually we rounded the delta's northeast corner, and steering southeast broke away from the shallows and headed across open water for the mainland. The wind was blowing southwest and working up a fair chop. Land was visible ahead, and we paddled toward it for a great long while. This stretch would have been very difficult in strong winds, and we were glad that the present winds were moderate.

We raised a tundra cliff, but paddle though we did, it seemed reluctant to draw near. Typically, from any distance we had no way of judging the height of such a cliff. This one could have been two feet or twenty. Eventually we found that it was about eight feet, which explained why we had paddled so long to reach it. Swinging northwest, we followed the shore, thankful to have negotiated the delta and for the security of higher land, inaccessible though it was at the moment because of the cliff. In another six miles we rounded a broad but clearly defined shoal at Drew Point, and from here could see the pack ice standing away to the north, maybe a mile away.

The sky cleared, the wind dropped, and we found ourselves paddling in idyllic conditions. After awhile we became so warm that we contemplated dropping our drysuits to the waists.

The reason we wore the drysuits was for safety in case of a capsize. "Dress for the water, not the air" is the sea-kayaker's axiom. Were it not for the cold water we would have worn much different clothing – clothing that breathed and allowed the perspiration to evaporate, and that would have allowed us to add layers or remove them as the conditions changed. But a capsize in such clothing could have been disastrous. At least in the drysuits, if the boat went over – due to our hitting something, or visa versa - we had a good chance of surviving the cold water and climbing back aboard.

Reaching a nice pull out, we stopped to cook lunch. As if on cue, the sky clouded over and an icy wind sprung from the north. Normally while in the kayak we were warm, except sometimes the hands and feet. The snug cockpits sheltered our lower bodies and legs, and the exercise of paddling kept our upper bodies warm. But on land we quickly chilled, since we were no longer generating metabolic warmth, and because our clothing was barely adequate for exposure to the frigid blast. The temperature had dropped so low that we could see our every exhalation. We huddled around the stove, and wolfed down a hasty pot of ground beef and corn spaghetti. The surf was beginning to pummel the shoreline and we had not a moment to lose, so we stuffed a handful of jellybeans into the front pocket of our drysuits, and set off again.

Soon the paddling had re-warmed us, and we continued following the coast, which here again was a series of high tundra cliffs up to twenty feet tall.

From the top of these cliffs, one would enjoy a commanding view of both sea and coastline. Apparently some of the local inhabitants appreciated this fact, also. First was a young fox, fluffy as a child's stuffed animal. Standing quite still, it watched us inquisitively for a few moments, then returned to its antics, leaping here then there, running one direction then back again, then suddenly freezing in place facing us, as though checking to see if we had been watching.

Next we paddled past caribou in groups of two or more, often standing at the edge of the bluffs where the strong wind blew away the insects. Then we spotted a snowy owl, silent and still as a statue – and surprisingly large, but again we lacked a frame of reference.

Now we paddled in fairly strong winds fine on the port bow. We were not too concerned, for the Arctic has its moods and we were starting to get used to them.

Eventually we reached another long line of cliffs, and I suggested that we stop and make camp, but Jenny was in favor of continuing. She wanted to see what was around the next point. But when we reached the end of the cliffs we both realized that we should have stopped. The shoreline ahead was quite low lying, and the headwinds had stiffened. That, and we were starting to flag.

Dogging ahead, we paddled past the towers of the Pitt Point Dew Line Station, which looked forlorn and alien in such a remote place.

Quite a ways farther we landed at 5:30 pm, and attempted to climb a four-foot sand bank. This was more difficult than it appeared because the sand slipped away and exposed slick ice that made the footing extremely dubious.

The terrain extending away to the south was lightly vegetated and segmented into roughly hexagonal tables maybe fifty feet across. Each table was separated by a four-foot-wide ditch, often filled with stagnant water. These tables are called tundra polygons, and are said to be common in the Arctic. They take centuries to develop, and are caused by the annual cycles of thawing and deep-freezing.

We selected a site on the sand not far from the shore bank. The entire region smelled like caribou, and in fact these animals were all around, watching us unload the boat. They were so graceful and beautiful to watch. They loved to run, and were swift and fluid. From a distance they looked like deer, but up close their rough-hewn heads reminded us more of moose. Most of the ones here lacked antlers, and many tended small calves.

While pitching the coliseum today we faced a new challenge. Normally when pounding in tent stakes, we managed to get them 8 or 12 inches into the ground before they struck permafrost, and this depth was ample for good strength. But here the ground was frozen so solid that we could not pound the stakes even a few inches. And the bags of gear inside the tent did not weigh enough to prevent the tent from blowing away. Once again we were confined to the tent, literally holding down the fort.

The sun returned, the wind slackened, and we spread things to dry: drysuits, life jackets, neoprene mitts and socks. Here we discovered areas of UV deterioration on the drysuit wrist gaskets. These gaskets for wrists and neck were made of a thin and stretchy latex, and the damage showed as faint cracks and stiffness. Eventually these areas would split. To defer that, we mixed a dab of sealant with several drops of accelerator, and painted on a thin film.

Day's Run: 36 n-mi, 12½ hrs. Camp: 70° 53.177' N, 153° 28.242' W

Day 55: July 29

The morning had brought rain, so we packed our drybags while still inside the tent, then dozed while waiting for a weather break.

Finally at 8:15 am we set off onto rough seas. The east-northeast winds at 12 to 15, fine on the port bow, made for slow and strenuous going.

Several miles further we reached the buildings of an ATCO site. This company operated the DEW line station, which looked to be about a 20 minute walk to the south. We had hoped to find water here, but could see no evidence of habitation. So rather than waste time scouting around, we continued on our way. Even though the weather was barely favorable, we needed to use it for making what miles we could.

Reaching Pitt Point we visited an old cabin that must have been a relic of the whaling era. The cabin was made mostly of hewn driftwood, with a wood floor and timbered roof covered in sod. The walls must have been sod-lined also, but now were bare and covered in pretty lichen. The interior was dank, and contained a number of artifacts including an old shoe, a

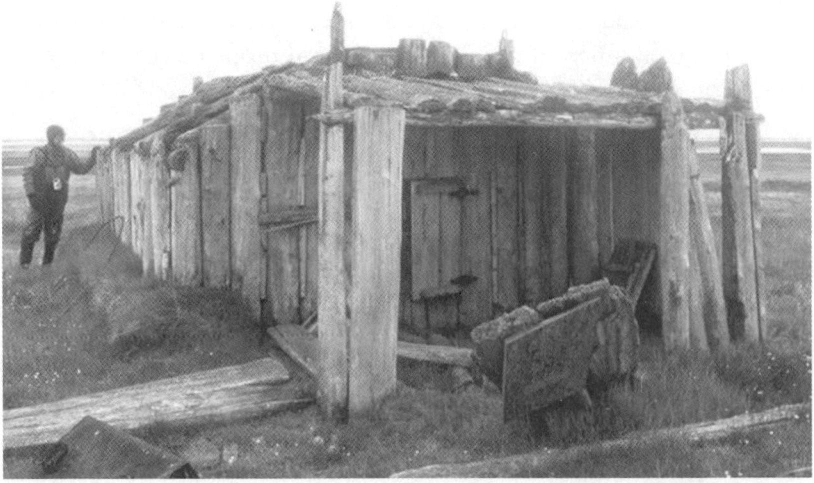

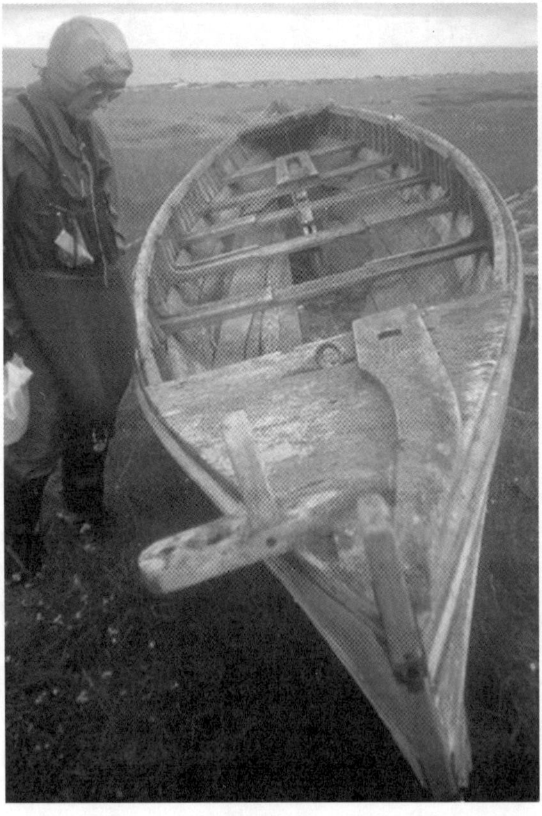

rusted saw, a stove in pieces, a sleeping cot, bookshelves, and so forth. Nearby was a pair of longboats. One was beautifully constructed and still in reasonable condition. All of this would have made a most interesting display in a museum.

This stretch of coast seemed to be favored by the geese, sea birds and shorebirds. So we had constant company: Canada and Brandt geese, plovers, glaucous gulls, kittiwakes, and a few others less familiar to us.

For some leg exercise Jenny lined the boat a ways. Here she startled a trio of fox that scampered warily away.

We were unable to correlate barometric fluctuations with changes in weather. However we did learn to recognize patterns in the sky.

Reaching land's end, we stopped to check our position and to input a few navigational coordinates. Then we paddled three miles of open water to Pagik Island. After following a chain of low and narrow islands - oversized sand bars, really - we jumped the four-mile gap back to the mainland.

Weary of paddling into stiff headwinds, we pulled ashore at 4:30 pm, about two miles short of Esook. Again today we had seen dozens of caribou. Here their tracks were everywhere, along with tracks of a bear in the mud just behind camp.

Day's Run: 17 n-mi, 8 hrs. Camp: 70° 52.949' N, 152° 40.812' W

Day 56: July 30

We awoke to find that the wind had ceased. Perfect silence. Peering outside, we found that the Arctic Ocean was lying strangely still. Overhead the sky was an inviting blue. Truly, all was well with the world - until we stepped outside and discovered a wall of fog speedily approaching from the north. This engulfed us within minutes.

Siku Kayak -- 179

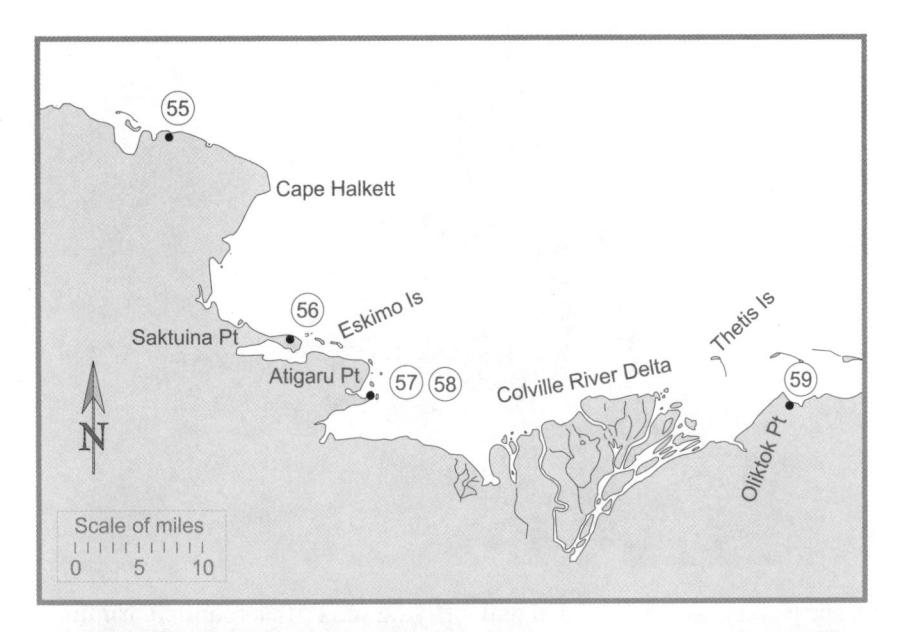

We set off at 6:30 am into a very chilly morning. Fog blowing off the polar ice pack is surely the world's best air conditioning. But as the wind piped up to 12 knots northeast, it felt more like the a polar deep freeze.

Just short of Cape Halkett we made a quick shore stop, and here we were the coldest of the entire trip, thus far. With our drysuits peeled to the waists, our clothing was woefully inadequate. Next time we determined to bring warmer insulated jackets and pants. But for now we were resigned to simply make do.

Cape Halkett was surrounded with offlying shoals that required paddling far around. But while working back to land in their lee we found flat water. The fog began to lift, and we enjoyed a very pleasant cruise southwest along the shore. Finally reaching the south end of the bay, we cut across three miles of open water and continued an additional few miles.

These ice-shelf shorelines were common along the top of Alaska

We landed for lunch near a large but strangely unidentifiable object on higher ground. We hiked far up the hill for some exercise, good views, and a closer inspection of what turned out to be a scraper - a large piece of machinery long since abandoned. Odd to see it standing forlornly out in the middle of nowhere. But in the imperceptible distance to the south was a large building, shown on the map as a landing strip.

The sun had come out, and we cooked a sumptuous pan of fried potatoes, sausage and eggs - as good as anything found in a restaurant, but unfortunately the last of these commodities for us. With backs to the wind and faces to the sun, the day was almost pleasant, as long as we did not dwell on the fact that we could easily see our breaths.

We happened to be huddled round our camp stove for its scant warmth when a noise startled us from behind. We turned and found a large-antlered caribou shuffling past, not three feet away. Dumbfounded, we watched it continue along the beach while paying us no heed.

Unfortunately our camera had been just out of reach. But as we were lamenting the missed photo, two more caribou wandered our way - a mother and her calf. This time we were ready. But they stopped a hundred feet short and lay down behind a log. Above them on the cutbank stood a young buck. This one continued moseying along the bank until directly above us. We remained still, and the buck - now just a few yards away and directly downwind - did not seem to notice us.

As we were packing, a few more caribou came wandering along the beach, going the other way. We were starting to feel invisible.

On the last of our arm power we paddled another four miles, and nearly to Saktuina Point stopped at 6:00 pm and made camp on the tundra about ten feet above the sea. The sun had come out in full force, so we spread things to dry, and sat back to revel in the beauty all around. The tundra extended as far as the eye could see, and was punctuated here and there with sparkling ponds and dotted with caribou grazing.

Ever since Barrow the coast had been tending southeast, so we had been ever so slowly gaining latitude. Now the banks were no longer vertical slices of permafrost and ice, at least not exclusively. Instead, they were starting to look more like normal banks. Here we also found the first willow in a long while. This was about their northern limit, and these mature bushes were hugging the ground practically flush.

Throughout the day we saw many hundreds of geese. The young ones were growing fast, and about half of them could fly. Perhaps in a few more weeks they would all be flying south.

I went for a long walk, shotgun in one hand and camera in the other. Just for fun I stalked three large caribou, and managed to approach within a few hundred feet. While not moving, I could stand there in plain sight without alarming them. They would look at me a while, then decide I was not a threat and go back to their grazing. With their heads down, I moved closer. Eventually I tired of the game and left them be.

Jenny fried a tasty round of pancakes, and we enjoyed sponge baths using water carried from one of the ponds.

Mosquito season seemed to have finished, for we had seen less than half a dozen in the week since departing Barrow. But then, neither had we experienced many warm and windless days for testing this theory. So far we had used less than half an ounce of insect repellent between us, thanks initially to the B vitamins, and then to our mosquito proof clothing and head nets.

Day's Run: 32 n-mi, 11½ hrs. Camp: 70° 35.104' N, 152° 04.675' W

Day 57: July 31

We awoke to find the wind calm and the sea flat. The top of the sleeping quilt was soaked in condensation, and the tent was covered in dew. This had been the case yesterday also. As we were breaking camp a northeast wind sprang forth, and within minutes a choppy sea was pummeling the beach. We set off at 7:30 am into stiff headwinds, and paddled a direct course for Eskimo Islands. We took a fair thrashing, but arrived in good shape. Both islands were as high as any mainland we had seen of late, maybe twenty feet, and on one of them stood a couple of caribou. This seemed odd, as the island was a couple miles from the mainland.

Paddling along the southern shoreline of both islands, we had to keep a ways off to avoid a few shoaling spits. Unfortunately the wind veered to east, then east-southeast, which again meant headwinds for the long open crossing back to the mainland.

We landed for a shore break and did our best to keep warm in the icy wind. Jenny often wore her neck ring in order to reduce the usual sweat-soaking of her clothing, but in open water this was not safe, so she arrived at this beach wearing a shirt that looked more like it had been dropped into the sea then wrung out. I helped her change into a dry shirt and don her parka. Then I took her for a brisk and warming walk. We found a nice pond, so returned to the boat for the water jug, bailer and filtration pump.

The boat carried two bailers, one tethered to each cockpit. Sometimes a wave would slosh unexpectedly over the deck and find its way into an open cockpit. For removing this water the bailer was quite handy. Mainly the bailers were for emergency. We could use them to empty the cockpits in the unlikely event of a capsize or swamping. But they served other purposes as well. One was a receptacle for urine, sometimes used in the kayak, and always kept by the tent's doorway at night. This bailer was of course clearly marked. The other bailer we used for collecting fresh water, such as today.

We had set off from Barrow six days ago with six gallons of drinking water. Now we were down to about half a gallon. One could probably have collected water from ponds all along the way, but because of the waterfowl thriving on those ponds, and the aquatic bugs in them, the water would best be filtered then boiled. Driftwood for boiling is abundant, but so is strong wind.

Warmth regained, or nearly so, we set off again, clawing our way into headwinds and eventually rounding Atigaru Point and its antenna tower. Here we became quite confused as to the lay of the coastline. What we saw with our eyes differed from what was shown on the map. Most predominately the map showed a large group of islands just offshore, but these we could not see. The problem was that as we sat in the boat, the height of eye was between two and three feet. And because the terrain was so low lying, anything more than a few miles away tended to hide below the horizon. And the higher parts of land looked like islands in an otherwise empty sea.

The strong east-southeasterly was an advantage in one respect, for the waves delineated the shoals and enabled us to steer well clear. A few miles farther south we landed ashore and climbed a ten-foot hill, and from that vantage found a way around another extensive shoal. From there another long open passage brought us back to land. The wind and seas were increasing, and we were uncertain of our exact position, but we suspected we were drawing close to the four-mile jump to the east/west coast of the mainland. We landed again at 2:00 pm and wandered around for some time while debating the proper course of action. Finally we decided that against our earnest desire for mileage, we had better make camp.

Something always seemed to characterize each day, and today it was the glaucous gulls. At this time of year they were extremely territorial and protective of their young. For an hour at a time they would dive on us with their scolding "ka-ka-ka-ka." Today they were particularly onerous, haranguing us for several more hours after we had made camp.

The beach here was covered in driftwood. Along much of the way we had seen a certain size of timber measuring about 8 inches by 12 inches by 15 feet long. With a good boat, one could have collected enough for a substantial cabin. We had also seen a large pile of these back at the Pitt Point ATCO site. Survey stakes were also becoming common amid the driftwood, and they made just about the best tent stakes imaginable.

Day's Run: 13 n-mi, 6½ hrs. Camp: 70° 29.980' N, 151° 41.938' W

Day 58: August 1

Stormbound in a strong east-southeast blow, we filtered three gallons of water, then built a campfire in the island's lee and boiled this water.

We were still perplexed by land to the south where none should have been, at least according to our maps and nautical chart. What we saw appeared to be an extensive sandbank about half a mile away. Finally, I realized that it was the mainland standing 4½ miles away. The Arctic has no end to its pranks.

A lone caribou came moseying our way, but one look at me and it retreated back along the mile-long sandbar angling north. As it went, the seagulls pestered it unmercifully. This was interesting. Once the gulls had accustomed to our presence, they actually served nicely as guard dog substitutes. Whenever they sounded the alarm, we knew to look.

Late afternoon a rainsquall drove us into the tent.

Day 59: August 2

At 5:45 am we embarked across a fairly calm sea. The sky was thickly overcast and the barometer down to 29.45. We paddled five miles on a diagonal toward the mainland, but nearing land we could not draw close because of shoals. We paddled east for eight miles to the shoals extending from the Colville River.

Because the Colville Delta is some 20 to 25 miles across, it constitutes a major obstacle for kayakers, what few of us there are. And for this crossing we were most fortunate to enjoy ideal weather, with flat seas and a mere breeze wafting from the northeast. We paddled north several miles in water a foot or less deep, and finding deeper water swung east and paddled five more miles to Tolaktuvot Point - the only place on the delta where one could land ashore.

En route, Jenny's drysuit neck gasket had split apart, meaning that her suit would be quite useless in the unlikely event of a capsize. We landed near an antenna, and I suggested she remove the suit so that we could repair it. But she wanted to press on, and fix it once we had cleared the delta.

The land here was fairly low lying, only two feet above the sea. And even though covered in grass it would not have been a good place to camp. So we paddled several miles northeast to shoal water, then swung the bow east. Here we were so far from land that it appeared as a dark line on the southern horizon. And even then it was not land, but extensive sandbars. The feeling was more like making a long, open crossing. The day had become positively hot, forcing us to strip our drysuits to the waists, only to be pestered by a few mosquitoes and black flies.

Like a phantom, an indistinct blob of land began slowly materializing ahead. I estimated aloud that it was probably our halfway point around the delta. We continued paddling with a will, but the landmarks, what few there were, remained fairly unchanging – as though we were caught in a strong countercurrent. We switched on Geepus, and he indicated our paddling speed at a hearty 4.3 knots. Still, for hour after hour we labored ahead, while the landmarks remained sluggish. This was because they were so far away, yet due to the lack of scale they did not look like it.

A shoal appeared to our left, and we took a position fix with Geepus and found ourselves 2½ miles south-southwest of Thetis Island. This meant we were past the delta, and five miles offshore. Geepus indicated that we were also 7½ miles from Oliktok Point, and the compass indicated that its bearing coincided with the bump of land we had been steering for all afternoon. So we continued on that heading, stroking across glassy seas. Using the monocular we were finally able to see that the bump was man-made. Still at quite a distance, it looked like a red submarine. To the right we could see the raydome of a DEW Line Station.

In another two hours we reached the sub - actually a huge building and possibly a desalination plant. As we drew near, a worker waved out his pickup window - our first human contact in a week. Welcome to the expansive Prudhoe Bay oil drilling and processing complex.

We paddled far past the building and landed ashore to determine our whereabouts. Again we were perplexed, mainly by a tower and bar to the east not shown on the maps. Probably man-made. Continuing on, we paddled southeast 1½ miles and at 6:15 pm landed at the base of a nice 4-foot bluff. We were so tired that we could hardly function; the result of having paddled for 12½ hours.

In brilliant sunshine we spread things to dry, and while Jenny cooked macaroni and cheese, and heated cuppas, I pitched the tent. A huge black cloud brought cold winds, and we had just managed to throw everything inside when the rains began. We were very pleased with the day's mileage of 51 nautical miles, which translates to 55.1 statute miles. This was the most ocean miles we had ever paddled in one day.

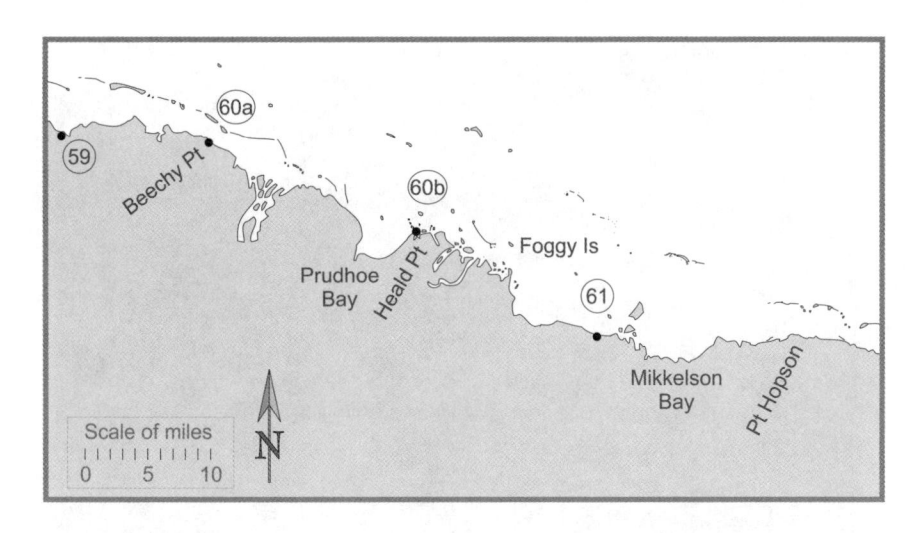

The storm left as quickly as it had come, and soon we were back outside gazing at the horizon to the north. Mirages were strangely raising the ice just beyond the sandbar islands. We patched Jenny's drysuit neck gasket with catalyzed sealant, which again did a remarkable job.

Day's Run: 51 n-mi, 12½ hrs. Camp: 70° 29.572' N, 149° 47.813' W

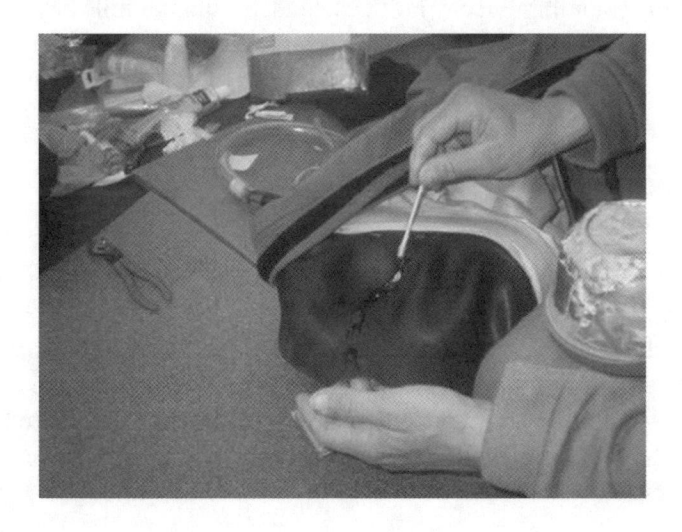

Day 60: August 3

Setting off at 7:30 am in a strong, east-northeast wind, eventually we reached what had originally appeared to be a very strange object, but which we now saw was a drilling tower surrounded by buildings. Steering directly across a bay to the next point of land, we paddled through its rip, then crossed a succession of bays, thus saving ourselves the extra effort and miles of following the crenulated shoreline. But the next three-mile bay beyond Milne Point was a wild ride amid breaking waves. So from Kaverak Point we followed the shoreline for safety.

Eventually rounding Beechy Point we landed a quarter mile beyond. The time was 11:30 am, and the wind was strong and laced with racing fog and slanting rain. We pitched the tent and crawled gratefully inside.

August 3, Morning stop. 16 n-mi, 4 hrs. Camp: 70° 28.890' N, 149° 09.101'W

August 3 continued

After a long nap we walked to the historic old cabin at Beechy Point. Two additions were still standing, but a third had plunged over the receding coastal bluff. The windows were boarded up and the interior dark as a cave. The door was open, and stepping inside we saw that the caribou had been sheltering here, and had made a terrible mess. A hundred yards beyond the cabin was another of newer vintage. A boat and snow machine there suggested that someone might be in residence, although we saw no one.

Back at the yak, Jenny cooked a hearty meal. Then we set off again at 7:00 pm, now in a light tailwind. The coast to Black Point was a ten-foot high sloping mud bank. Once beyond that, and the Sakonowuak River, we steered east, out into Gwydyr Bay while taking a wide course around the Kuparuk (*kuh PUH ruk*) River delta. For about nine miles we stayed well out, and eventually reached a man-made causeway leading far out to an oil rig. Fortunately this causeway had a bridge about one mile offshore, and this saved us perhaps four miles of going out and around. Beneath this bridge the current was flowing quite strongly going our way. We landed momentarily for a view from the slightly higher vantage. Nearby was a small modular building with a bright red sign reading "Warming Station" and two oversized doors, one reading "Enter" and the other "Exit."

Continuing a ways south into Prudhoe Bay proper, we steered a course across it six miles. Now midnight, the sky was aglow with twilight. The scattered structures with their thousands of electric lights brought to mind some sort of futuristic Las Vegas on the backside of the moon.

We powered across the bay casting occasional glances at a huge cloud rolling in from behind and threatening to rake the sea into dangerous combers. Fortunately the waves grew no larger than 1½ feet. The dim twilight made visibility especially difficult, so we were glad to finally reach shore. Rounding a small point, we landed at 1:00 am (Aug 4), very satisfied with the nearly 100 statute miles covered in the past two days.

Carrying our things up an eight-foot bank to the tundra grass, we could see the ice clearly visible in horizon mirages raised behind offlying sandbars. Turning around and looking inland, the oil complexes still shone across the darkened tundra, with their myriad electric bulbs glowing a pale, sickly orange.

Day's Run: 38 n-mi, 10 hrs. Camp 70° 20.332' N, 148° 14.539' W

Day 61: August 4

Rising at 7:30 am, we had just started packing when two people came walking across the tundra. Tom and Dave said that they had been waiting for us to appear, as they were leery of being mistaken for a bear prowling around outside the tent, knowing that we probably had a gun. Tom was wearing a Security Guard uniform, and by the looks on both their faces we guessed we were about to be chewed out. But they were friendly, and the lecture was mild. It seems that visitors to the Prudhoe area were unwelcome. Ostensibly this was for safety reasons. The fellows explained that hydrogen sulfide gas escapes from the wells, and can reach toxic concentrations during periods of calm. We later learned that the gas is caused when the drillers inject ordinary pond water into the shafts, as a means of achieving greater oil yield. The bacteria in the pond water reacts with the sulfurous petroleum compounds, to produce the poisonous gas.

Tom took our picture - with his camera not ours - and asked for our names and address. He instructed us not to land on the Endicott Causeway, and also recommended we avoid any native cold storage lockers - pits dug in the ground long ago - due to possible gas concentrations.

Tom said he had lived here for 18 years, and Dave for 15. They asked about our trip and whether we had seen any polar bears. They were interested in these animals due to their risk to the workers. They said the previous summer they had seen 17 polar bears. They explained that these animals tended to come ashore when the north wind blew the pack ice in. These were mainly juveniles "looking for their niche," having been ousted by the older and larger males. But sometimes the wind would change and blow the ice away, leaving the bears stranded. While waiting for the ice to return, the bears would go into "walking hibernation," prompted by the lack of food on shore. They are strongly attracted by smells, Tom said, and would investigate anything that is not snow white. He said that after the whale hunters from Kaktovik and other villages inland had finished butchering at Cross Island, the polar bears would move in by the droves.

We set off at 8:30 am and paddled past a facility at Heald Point, then steered direct for another large plant at the far end of the causeway. Shoal water intervened, and required us to paddle half a mile north, from where we found deeper water all the way to the tip of the causeway. Each of these facilities was enormous, especially from the low vantage of a kayak. And everything was strictly industrial.

We had been paddling 10 to 12 knot quartering tail winds from the southwest, so were glad to finally pull into the man-made island's lee. The only people in evidence were three or four workers. And when they waved to us, we realized they might be security guards watching to make sure we did not land.

Continuing three miles east across open water in light airs, we landed ashore at Point Brower for a quick stop. On the beach Jenny found a plastic disk, about 6-inch diameter, dispatched from the University of Alaska. The disk was imprinted with the message: $1 reward for return of the serial number and location found. We thought it strange that an accredited science project would litter the landscape.

Paddling under blue skies and across uncharacteristically glassy Beaufort seas, we crossed the open reaches of Foggy Island Bay. The Brooks Range stood silhouetted clearly in the distance ahead, while out at sea the polar pack gleamed white across the horizon. The afternoon became very hot, so Jenny unzipped her drysuit while I removed mine entirely. We were taking in the views when what first appeared as a small dark speck on the water turned out to be a seal swimming with its head out of the water. We drew within a hundred feet, and for 10 or 15 seconds it stared at us, then plunged beneath the surface.

A southeast wind encouraged more vigor in finishing the 5-mile crossing, and we eventually landed at an old campsite of some sort. It featured a small plywood cabin and nearby a couple of tent platforms. We guessed it was an archeologist's camp.

Now in increasing headwinds we lined the yak a mile or two, then stopped for lunch. Exploring the region we found several tufts of qiviut, the inner fur of the muskox. This fur is shed naturally in summer, and the previous summer we had collected quite a lot from the willows where the animals had brushed against them.

Eventually we decided to quit the battle. The headwinds had become very strong and the seas heavily white capped. So at 4:00 pm we climbed an eight-foot bank and made camp.

Exploring a few hundred yards inland we found what looked like an old grave. It was a wooden structure resembling an upturned boat, with hewn timbers carefully placed. It looked like a vestige of the whaling era. The permafrost prevents a proper burial beneath the ground, so a structure like this would have protected the grave from marauding animals.

Day's Run: 22 n-mi, 7½ hrs. Camp: 70° 11.549' N, 147° 26.611' W

Day 62: August 5

In the early morning we awoke to find the tent soaked with dew, and its contents wet with condensation. We set off at 5:45 am, admiring stunning views of the Brooks Range "sawing savage at the sky." The wind was light northwest and veering to northeast. The Shaviovik River required us to paddle far offshore in shallows. So once into Mikkelson Bay we found ourselves miles offshore. The shore of this bay was generally high-banked, and was to be the last of its kind. Ahead, the shores were lower, and made not of mud and sand, but gravel. Even the land extending inland was to become much lower. The sky to the south and west was black, and the day was starting to chill.

Siku Kayak -- 199

The Bullen Point DEW Station was the first one we had seen built close to the sea. It appeared to have been long since abandoned, but curiously the helicopter pad lights were on. Soon a helicopter landed, and someone waved from the cockpit as we paddled past. To us this felt almost like meeting someone from a future century, so different was his world from ours.

A few hours later, half way between Points Hopson and Sweeney, we stepped ashore and built a warming fire of driftwood. Even though I was wearing three pairs of heavy wool socks, my feet were nearly numb. This was mainly because the socks had absorbed excessive condensation during the night, caused by the tent's inadequate ventilation. Any tent, even one with large vents, will collect and condense internal moisture;

and this moisture saps body heat. But the hot fire dried the socks, warmed our feet, drove away the chill, and provided heat under the frying pan for Jenny's delicious pancakes. No wonder we humans have such an affinity for campfires. Setting off again half an hour later, we felt much revived.

A few miles beyond Point Thompson was what appeared to be an abandoned oil well structure. In ten knots northwest we jumped three miles to Flaxman Island, and drew near shore near an old cabin. Here was another helicopter with its engine running. Even though we paddled within a few hundred feet, this pilot seemed not to notice us. His machine had the colors of the BP Oil Company - green and yellow, while the first one had been ARCO red and blue.

Another three-mile open passage took us to a large spit extending from the island's southeast corner. Rounding the spit we came to a long line of ice standing just offshore, presumably grounded. We landed and found the spit actually consisted of large rocks, the first rocks we had seen in weeks.

We started walking inland with the intent of climbing a 15 or 20-foot hill for a better view of the way ahead. The ground showed many tracks of muskox. But when Jenny found a fresh bear track – very fresh and perhaps a polar bear - we judiciously returned to the boat.

Fog enshrouded the way ahead and hid the spit extending from Brownlow Point. So we paddled the mile and a half gap on a compass bearing, and fortunately this took us directly to the spit. Paralleling the sandbar, we noticed a recent hunters' campsite, as indicated by extra-long tent pegs pounded into the sand, and several caribou antlers lying about.

The ice was a scant fifty to a hundred yards offshore, and because of the fog we could not tell how far the ice extended northwards. We paddled past an abandoned radar site, where the storms and surf had undermined one building. The region was littered with 55-gallon barrels. Beyond was another old cabin.

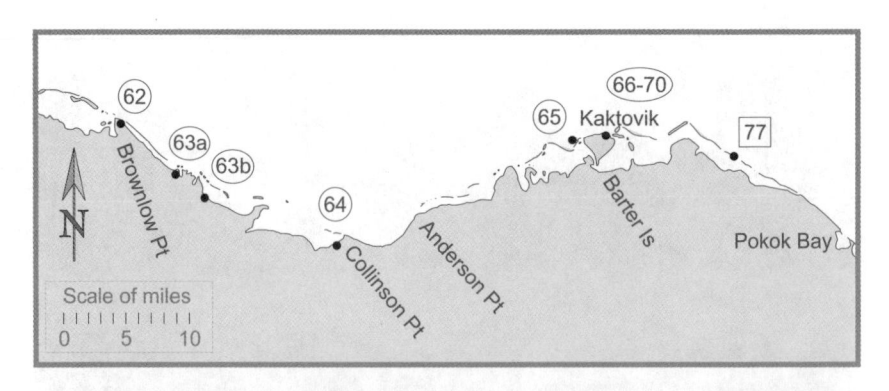

Cotton grass

Eleven hundred miles into our summer's journey, we relax on the tundra-covered shore of the Beaufort Sea.

At 4:45 pm we landed between the two structures. The cold and fog made the place seem a bit dismal, but the coliseum provided the needed comfort and warmth.

We had seen no animals today, but did observe many large flocks of pintail ducks, cheery little plovers, and what Jenny referred to as "flying frogs." These were loons, and to my ears, as well, they did croak rather like frogs as they flew overhead.

Day's Run: 39 n-mi, 11 hrs. Camp: 70° 09.727' N, 145° 50.738' W

Day 63: August 6

Setting off at 6:30 am, we followed the outside of the sandbar, steering well clear of the occasional patch of shoals because the hard gravel seabed could have damaged the hull. The wind was westerly, which put it on our starboard quarter. The morning was quite foggy and for a while we could not see much ice. But later when the fog cleared we could see it everywhere. Our shore lead was only a hundred yards wide.

In a mile we came to a pass, and here we entered a lagoon that offered respite from the strong winds abeam. A quick shore break and we were back out again, following the mainland shore comprising mostly six-foot mud bluffs indented with a number of puntas. Rounding one point into its quiet lee, we would cut the bay by only one-third and paddle open water to the far shore. Next we would hug the shore to the succeeding point, before making the next jump across. In a few places we encountered offlying rocks barely awash. Some were quite jagged and could have damaged the yak. The waves were clearly identifying most of them, but we did miss one by only a few inches, at speed.

The wind was increasing and fanning the bays into gnarly whitecaps, and once we reached the Tamayariak River delta we decided we had better land ashore for safety, and make camp. While grinding along a final line of bluffs, we encountered shoals that called for a beeline toward shore, and we soon found ourselves working through only 3 or 4 inches of water.

At 9:30 am we landed and found a suitable place to pitch the tent in our usual manner in such high winds: by positioning the yak just upwind and securing a pair of lines to the tent to prevent it from blowing away. But while I was lifting the tent clear of the ground, so that Jenny could position the ground sheet, a pole snapped from the strain of the wind. This was where we learned not to pick up the tent by its poles mid-span, but only from both ends.

Un-chocking the poles we flattened the tent to the ground. Removing the broken pole, I spent the next 40 minutes effecting the repair, hampered by the near freezing gale. A pity the manufacturer had not included a couple of repair sleeves, as we had requested. The pole segment had snapped two inches from one end, precisely over the end of the internal insert. This insert had obviously created a stress riser because it was not tapered. Moreover, we found that the pole end was cracked and that this crack led directly to one of the sleeve-retainer punch-marks. Obviously the pole had been punched in its heat-treated condition, creating even more stress.

I removed the sleeve from its broken piece and glued it into the end of another pole piece. Then I positioned the broken pole at one end of the chain and into it inserted the end-ferrule. That way the ragged end would not cause problems. Thus, the pole regained its original strength, but lost two inches of length.

By the time we had re-pitched the tent and secured it with stakes all around, we were more than ready to climb in and escape the icy blast. But first we had to find water, since our supply had nearly run out. Carrying rifle, water bottle, bailer, and water filter, we hiked up a gradual slope across grassy marshlands and soon came to a number of ponds. From the deepest one we filtered 2½ gallons of quite good looking and good tasting water.

Back at the tent we crawled gratefully inside and were soon fast asleep beneath the quilt.

August 6, morning stop. 8 n-mi, 3 hrs. Camp 70° 04.750' N, 145° 34.608'W

August 6 continued

Anxious to make more miles, when the wind decreased to manageable proportions we packed up and set off at 8:00 pm. While paddling around the Tamayariak River we glanced occasionally at the pack ice lying a mile further out.

Unfortunately, the lull was only temporary. For the next 1½ hours we labored into stiff headwinds, watching the clouds thickening and darkening the night. This darkness made visual navigation difficult. And because the irregular terrain kept us well out, we had trouble finding a suitable place to land. The storm was intensifying and by the time we reached shore at 1:00 am, now August 7, whitecaps were festering the sea.

After making a few trips up the six-foot embankment with our gear, we carried the kayak together as usual – one at each end. Then we spent the next 15 minutes searching for a suitable place to camp on the uneven and soggy tundra. That found, we pitched the tent and collapsed inside.

Day's Run: 15 n-mi, 5 hrs. Camp: 70° 02.207' N, 145° 26.351' W

Day 64: August 7

Strong winds persisted most of the day, so we slept several extra hours. Fatigue was starting to catch up with us, mainly because of our meager food intake. We were not cooking at our camps because of the risk of bears, and were nearly out of non-cook food.

For several hours a jaeger flew around, as though nesting somewhere nearby. We had seen these birds all along the coast from Shishmaref, and had always found them interesting. Jaegers hunt for eggs, small birds and mammals, fish and even insects. They also have a pesky habit of stealing food from other birds, and time and again we had observed these aerial skirmishes.

Suddenly there came an explosion. It sounded like a gunshot at close range. I grabbed the rifle and leapt outside, only to find ourselves quite

Jaeger stealing food from a gull.

alone on the vast stretch of tundra. My next thought was that the permafrost beneath the tent might have cracked. We were camped fairly close to the edge, and these cracks were common. Then we discovered the cause - another broken tent pole.

This time the break was not due to strong wind, for the wind had by now lessened. Rather, it was the several weeks of cold and wind-induced vibration that together had been creating stress fatigue.

The break occurred to the same pole that had snapped before, but at a different place. Again it was at the end of a sleeve, near the tent's apex. From a design standpoint this pole needed to be factory pre-bent prior to hardening, to lessen the stress. And again, the location of the fracture indicated a stress riser caused by a non-tapered sleeve. We removed the broken pole, but did not repair it this time because the tent seemed to function nearly as well without it.

The wind continued to abate, so at 8:00 pm we set off, and paddled along the coast to Konganevik Point. Then heading south-southeast across the bay, in three miles we arrived back at the mainland. Overhead the clouds were very dark, while away to the south a moiling scud was obscuring the Brooks Range, but allowing an occasional glimpse of its lower flanks. In the past several days we had been admiring these mountains with their snow-capped peaks. The way they rose abruptly from the tundra plains is fairly typical of the Rockies when viewed from the east.

While plying the coast we saw two snowy owls, each about a mile apart. Owls are fascinating birds, and the large snowy owls in their brilliant

Driven ashore by a fast-approaching gale, as the midnight sun peeks beneath ominous clouds.

white robes are especially so. We had found a few of their feathers, one with pretty brown splotches.

Despite what the maps indicated, the shoals of the Katakturak River required paddling out and around. That done, we had to paddle east-southeast a long ways back to the mainland. This time, however, the wind was dead astern, so we sped along on a wild mouse ride, surfing occasionally and straining to reach the safety of shore without mishap.

We landed at 11:45 pm near Collinson Point. Even though the mud bank was about 30 feet high, the tundra above was still very wet. Searching the area at length, we finally found a suitable place and had nearly completed pitching the tent when squishing sounds beneath our feet suggested we move the tent elsewhere. When one first stepped on this ground it seemed dry enough, but the longer one stood there the more the tundra sank and the soggier it became. We carried the tent to a drier place and finished pitching it – still minus its broken pole.

Day's Run: 18 n-mi, 4 hrs. Camp: 69° 57.865' N, 144° 53.448' W

Day 65: August 8

At 5:30 am we set off again. The winds were light but frigid, and the sky completely clouded. Paddling directly across the bay, we rounded the sandbar to the east of Collinson Point. Reaching Marsh Creek we found that, contrary to its name, it was a sparkling, nicely flowing river and one of the best sources of drinking water we had seen all summer. We paddled upstream a hundred yards and landed on a gravel bar, and there filtered a supply of water into our jugs.

Paddling along the shore of Camden Bay, almost to Anderson Point we landed ashore and built a campfire. Primarily this was for drying clothing and sleeping quilt. But also we used it for frying pancakes. Driftwood was in plentiful supply, and ranged from small twigs to logs 75 feet in length. All this had been washed out of the rivers. Yet oddly, birch bark rolls were very few. So we usually started our fires with shavings cut from driftwood. Our folding knife had a serrated blade that cut quickly.

From Barrow the coastline angles gradually more south, so we expected to find a little more warmth. Instead, the days had become progressively colder. And because of the constant cloud cover and heavy dew factor at night, our tent with its limited ventilation had been taxing our clothing and quilt to their limits. We were struggling almost constantly to keep warm. In fact, for most of the previous night we had been deeply chilled.

Earlier in the trip we had used our parkas as pillows, but now wore them beneath the quilt. And even then, they were so damp that they provided little extra warmth. So today's campfire was a welcome opportunity to dry things, and to enjoy the hot meal.

At this point we had traveled more than two weeks beyond our last grocery store, and were down to one meal a day, if that. Clearly, we needed fresh food. This would have kept nicely in this naturally refrigerated climate. Jenny's homemade jerky had been a tasty snack, but we had long since eaten the last of it.

Rounding Anderson Point we paddled far out around the Sadlerochit River. Then we plied the open ocean for seven miles to the mouth of the Hulahula River. This was quite a large delta and paddling around it entailed another seven miles of open but shallow water. I was feeling ill; something seemed to be coming on. But I also knew that we could not afford to waste such good weather. Offshore, the pack ice was very thick, and we had to paddle within half a mile of it all the way to Arey Island.

Along the way we stopped for a quick break. Emerging from the boat we stood in mid-calf-deep water. This felt extremely odd because we were probably three miles from shore. Looking at the kayak floating in what looked like mid ocean, it seemed almost like a space ship, our life source and only means of returning to terra firma.

Nearly to Arey Island we were cut off by an offlying sand bar, with shoals blocking from the side. But the bar was only five feet wide, easily portaged, and we soon gained deeper water in the shore lead.

Reaching Arey Island we found the shoreline cluttered with floes, mostly car-sized slabs of ice that had drifted in. We landed for a rest, and although

350 miles east of Barrow on Arctic Alaska's north coast.

I was tired and would have rather crawled into the tent, this would not have been a good place to camp because of its lack of higher ground.

By now a stiff northerly was blasting frigid spray, and the fog was moving in. We followed the long, narrow island to its end. From there our chart indicated we should paddle due north to the spit extending southwest from Barter Island. Our two additional maps indicated the same thing. This was perplexing, because we could see no land to the north, and the shape and size of the waves suggested there was none. We later realized that Arey Island was segmented, and that where we stood had appeared to be its end, but was only a large gap not shown on the chart or maps.

We could see Barter Island in the distance to the east, so took our chances and paddled in that direction a couple of miles. Wending among floes we finally landed on another bar at 4:30 pm.

Exactly which bar this was, I was not quite sure. But one thing I did know: I needed to get out of the wind immediately. I started pulling gear from the boat's compartments, and asked Jenny for help in pitching the tent. She was incredulous because we were within four miles of the village. But when I told her I was in the initial throes of another malarial relapse, she understood.

Once inside, Jenny broke out a chemical warming packet, one of three we carried for emergencies. It was imperceptibly slow in starting, but after an hour it put out a surprising amount of heat, and this lasted the next eight hours.

Day's Run: 25 n-mi, 11 hrs. Camp: 70° 06.821' N, 143° 46.701' W

Siku Kayak -- 213

Fog and ice floes welcome us to Barter Island.

Snow dusts our camp outside the village of Kaktovik,
the only village on Alaska's north shore.

Day 66: August 9

With the worst behind me, we broke camp and set off at 10:00 am. I could have used more rest, but even more essential now was wholesome food. The trip from Barrow had taken eighteen days, and our food bags were so empty that we were practically running on fumes.

In fresh headwinds we paddled among scattered floes, and found that they actually benefited progress by blocking some of the wind and reducing the waves.

Following the gravel bar we reached Barter Island proper, and proceeded along its 30-foot high mud banks. The airport building came into view, and at 11:30 am we landed near the end of the bank fronting the village. Making camp on the gravel beach at the base of the mud bank, we hoped for at least a few hours of peace before the villagers discovered us.

Jenny headed into town, and soon returned with a few sacks of groceries. She was about to start cooking when her stove sputtered to a halt. The unleaded gasoline from the gas station at Barrow may have been of suspect purity, for the stove's needle jet had been clogging on occasion. But soon I had the stove purring nicely again, and Jenny cooked a delicious breakfast of potatoes, sausage and eggs.

Exploring the area behind camp, we found an old Inupiaq "refrigerator." This was a hole dug deep in the ground and equipped with a makeshift ladder. The hole had long since filled in with clumps of tundra.

That night a storm dusted the region in its first snow, and drove the pack ice right to the beach – making further kayaking impossible. We had barely made it to Kaktovik.

Day's Run: 3 n-mi, 1½ hrs. Camp: 70° 08.004' N, 143° 37.079' W

Days 66-71: August 9-14 Kaktovik

Early morning I accompanied Jenny to the laundromat. There we met Loren Ahlers and his adopted Inupiat daughter Crystal. For many years Loren had worked at the Barter Island DEW Line Station, in maintenance, he said. He married a native woman and had recently built a house here and settled down. Crystal was about 10 years of age, and she kindly helped us with our laundry.

Later in the morning we met several other villagers. They were so friendly and welcoming that we began to feel at home here in Kaktovik.

We were walking back toward camp with heavy resupply boxes, when a native fellow pulled his 4-wheeler to a stop and offered to help. Placing the boxes on the rear rack and securing them with bungees, he invited Jenny to take the rear seat. Then he drove her to our camp while I walked. Discovering our boat, he uttered the word "kayak!" and gave a long, rising and falling whistle. Daniel Akootchook, a retired whaling captain, had a keen interest in such boats.

Wind blowing off the nearby pack ice made the day especially frigid. We had been in the tent about 15 minutes when we heard Daniel's 4-wheeler returning. Looking out, we saw that he was towing a small trailer. "You move into my house," he offered. "It's cold out here!" We expressed appreciation, but assured him that we were comfortable here in our tent. He warned us of a big storm approaching, but by the glimmer in his eyes we figured he was bluffing. But when he warned us of Nanook, we knew he was serious - still, we figured we would take our chances. Well then, he reasoned, if we would not budge, then at least we must come to his house for a visit. "It gets lonely," he said, "since the kids moved out." We asked how many he had. With a subtle grin that seemed to be his hallmark, he tried counting on the fingers of both hands a few times. Then in a joking manner he shrugged his shoulders and said, "I don't know!" Half a dozen times he explained which house was his, making sure we would soon come for a visit.

Daniel's house was a typical Inupiaq dwelling, frame construction and not unlike those found in many lower-income regions in the lower 48. The yard was cluttered in what might have been taken as junk, things that would have filled a garage had there been one.

The village did not seem to have many dogs, but Daniel had two, which he said belonged to one of his children. Queenie and 7-Up were not your usual city-type dogs. They were enormous Inupiaq work and sled animals, and we soon discovered that anyone unsuspecting enough to approach closer than the ends of the dog's taut chains was practically mauled with affection. An Inupiaq dog is bred for work and does not know how to stand there quietly and accept a friendly pat on the head.

Entering the house, one was struck by a sweet but vaguely unpleasant odor that we later identified as dried walrus meat. These animals are not common along this part of the coast, but the hunters manage to take the occasional one. The entry was lined both sides with extraordinarily heavy jackets and coveralls hanging from the walls, and massive boots on the floor. A second doorway led to the living room, where Daniel's wife Lillian greeted us and offered us hot chocolates.

Lillian returned to her small couch with its overstuffed pillows and knitted afghan, and resumed work on a new pair of leather gloves she was making for herself and decorating in beadwork butterflies. Photos of the children and grandchildren hung on the wall behind her.

The living room was chock-a-block with well-worn furniture, overflowing bookshelves, interesting knickknacks, and a couple of small tables stacked high with magazines, newspapers, videos, and who knows what else.

During our stay at Kaktovik, the polar ice pack moved right against the shore. We took this photo from our camp.

Against one wall were the TV and VCR, and next to Daniel's chair was the CB radio.

In contrast to its rough, weather-worn appearance externally, the interior was cozy and warm. In fact, extremely warm. The villagers heated their homes with diesel, and they liked it turned up high. To us it bordered on stifling.

Daniel and Lillian regaled us with stories of village life, and in particular the whaling. After a bit of searching they found an hour-long video that Daniel had taken during a previous season's whale hunt. As the video played, our hosts narrated, and we watched fascinated as the Inupiaq captured a bowhead.

Daniel pulled out a small device of some sort, and started clicking it against various parts of his shoulders and arms. I asked what it was, and he explained that it was a piezoelectric sparker. He positively swore by the thing, saying that it really did cure various problem areas. I wondered aloud if it would work on my torn trapezius muscle of the shoulder, the result of once lifting a much too heavily laden kayak. This injury had been bothering me the past few years, mainly whenever I paddled. Borrowing Daniel's device I administered about a dozen sparks to the area. The problem seemed to vanish. It never bothered me again.

On the invitation of Daniel and Lillian, the next day we attended church, and were surprised to find that Daniel played the 12-string guitar in accompaniment to the singing. The preacher spoke mainly Inupiaq, but occasionally recapitulated in broken English. Part of his message was that when going on a rough ride, we must hang on and know that God is there helping us.

The service concluded with a breakfast of sausages rolled in pancakes, courtesy of the local tourist lodge, the Waldo Arms. Here we met the friendly Waldo owners, Merlyn Traynor and her husband Walt Audi. We asked if they had a supply of paperback books for possible trade – most such lodges do - and they said sure, bring ours by anytime.

As we walked outside, Daniel asked about the boat ride we were going on. He was always making little jokes designed to confuse the unwary, and we had no idea what he was talking about, until Lillian asked if we would like to go for a picnic in their boat. We said "Sure, we'd love to." Lillian became excited, and by this we knew the trip promised to be fun.

Figuring out how to drive Daniel's 4-wheeler

To expedite matters, Daniel suggested we drive his 4-wheeler to our camp, to pick up whatever things we needed. The machine was fun to drive, and it handled the soft beach sand with surprising agility.

Back at the house we piled the 4-wheeler with big coveralls and fir-lined parkas, and loaded its trailer with tanks of extra gasoline and a cooler of food.

The small harbor was beautifully protected in the nearby lagoon, and here we found a few dozen skiffs, including Daniel's Boston Whaler and 80 hp outboard. Lillian doled out the massive garments for everyone to

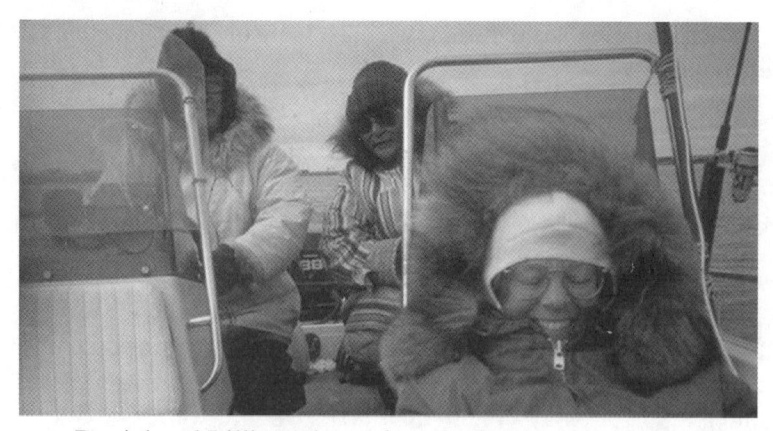

Daniel and Lillian take us for a boat ride and picnic.

put on, warning that the boat ride would be extremely cold. Suitably bundled, we were directed to take the front seats.

In contrast with the ice-choked Beaufort Sea, the expansive Jago Lagoon was mostly clear. Whizzing across its surface at ten times our kayaking speed, we quickly realized the worth of the heavy garments. The blast was penetratingly cold. Heading east for 15 or 20 miles, Daniel skillfully navigated around occasional shoals while avoiding a few scattered floes. The ride was exhilarating, and we saw a few other boaters out enjoying the rare spell of fine weather also.

Pulling up to a long sandbar, we anchored the boat and wandered to a nearby sod dwelling. Daniel said that when he had first moved to Kaktovik from Barrow back in the early 1940's, people were living in this dwelling. He said he was born in Barrow in 1933. As we were strolling along the beach, Lillian collected a few choice pieces of cottonwood bark for carving model canoes, and some diamond willow, which she said made beautiful woodcarvings because it took a nice polish. Pointing at the occasional flow, she suggested that this one resembled a dragon, that one a ship, and so forth. Jenny and I chuckled because while paddling among the floes our imaginations had run much the same course.

After visiting a second sod house, which the storms had mostly filled with sand, we returned to the skiff and enjoyed a picnic on the beach. Lillian had found a piece of plywood, and on this she spread the food. We all sat on the ground around it. Lillian poured hot soup from a vacuum flask, and offered me a piece of walrus. I bit into it, but my teeth barely made indentations. "Use this knife," she explained, "and put some butter on it." The walrus was strong flavored and the butter did not seem to help. But they also had caribou, and to me this tasted much better. Daniel had shot the caribou a few weeks ago, by happenstance at Brownlow Point where we had seen antlers on the beach. He and Lillian had dried the meat by hanging big chunks on a rack. They had not dehydrated the meat completely, but left it still somewhat soft on the inside.

While in Kaktovik we also visited with a few other residents. The following evening we enjoyed a home-cooked meal at the home of postmaster Harris Yang. He had worked as a professional chef, and the meal was as sumptuous as one might have found in an expensive Anchorage restaurant.

We stopped by the Waldo Arms to trade our paperback books, and found that they served tasty and inexpensive meals. There we met Vern Tejas, a rugged Alaskan mountain climber of no little renown. The three of us shared a table and talked about life here in the far north. Vern was working for the summer as a marine electronics technician, and he generously paid for our lunch.

Now and again Daniel would drop by our camp to check on us, but otherwise we had the beach essentially to ourselves. The danger of pilfering seemed non-existent, so we were able to walk into town or explore the adjacent areas at will.

While wandering a ways east of town we found a broken and discarded fishing pole. It was made of carbon fiber, and I figured it would be just the thing for making tent pole repair sleeves. Back at camp I used my miniature hacksaw blade to cut the pole into a few 6" lengths. With one of these I repaired the broken tent pole. Still in an industrious mood, I used silicone to waterproof our drysuit booties, which were starting to show the effects of the scores of miles walked in them.

Day 71: August 14

When arriving in Kaktovik we were of a mind to end the summer's journey and return home. This had not been an unreasonable plan, considering that we were fairly exhausted, mainly from living and paddling in the frigid climate, and from the prolonged lack of nutrition associated with the vast distances between villages. Also, the steadily dropping temperatures suggested that the season was drawing to a close. But more importantly, the polar pack had closed in so tightly that the chances of pushing ahead seemed slim. Accordingly, we had made travel arrangements for ourselves and transport for the boat. The yak would fly to Anchorage via air cargo (one flight every 2 or 3 weeks on a DC6 or Herc). Another option would have been to barge it to Prudhoe, then truck it to Anchorage with NAC. We ourselves planned to fly to Fairbanks.

However, in these 4½ days the pack had moved a ways back out, and the good meals along with plenty of rest, had revived us. So we were now eager to attempt the final leg of our summer's journey, from Barter Island to Inuvik.

Originally we had hoped to reach the coastal village of Tuktoyuktuk, but the intervening town of Inuvik lies quite a distance up the Mackenzie River, and this would probably remain ice free for at least another month. So Inuvik seemed like a much better bet.

All well and good, but we were not about to make the same mistake we had in Barrow, setting off with so little food. This time we had enough fresh food for two weeks, and enough dry food for an additional two weeks. This filled the yak's center compartment to overflowing. The remainder we had to stow in the cockpits and carry in our laps.

The morning was early when we set off - 5:30 am - and unfortunately the spell of good weather was drawing to a close, although we were hopeful in its return. But for now we paddled beneath dark and brooding clouds in a light southwest wind. Once past the airport we ducked into Jago Lagoon and enjoyed quite a few miles of ice-free water. But because it was ice free, it was also fairly rough.

The lagoon did not go on forever, and eventually we had to exit through a wide break in the bar. The open ocean was heavily laden in floes, and while looking far ahead we could hardly see a way among them. But they were usually surrounded by at least some open water, all but a few large patches that required us to steer far around. Surprisingly, by 10:30 am we had gone well past our picnic site, as indicated by Geepus. We landed just past Griffin Point for a quick shore break, then in light drizzle continued wending among the floes.

Beyond Angon Point we ducked into the Beaufort Lagoon, and paddled a few more miles to a headland. Here we made camp at 2:45 pm on a gravel and sand bar at the base of an eight-foot bank. We slept through the remaining afternoon to the patter of rain.

Day's Run: 35 n-mi, 9¼ hrs. Camp: 69° 54.593' N, 142° 20.038' W

226 -- *Siku Kayak*

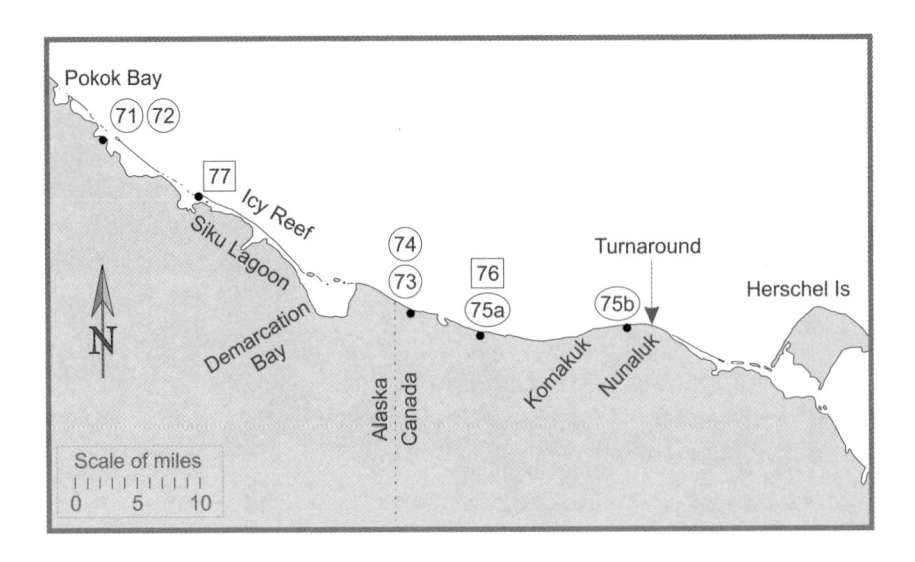

Day 72: August 15

Gnarly weather kept us tent-bound all day, with rain and what would have been headwinds. Another trepidation was the nearly 30 miles of hyphenated bar we would have to paddle along before reaching terra firma. For traversing this stretch we felt we needed a good day. So we slept, read, and nibbled on snacks, then finally walked half a mile around the corner to cook a large breakfast of potatoes, sausage and eggs. The fog was thick but we knew the wind was blowing the ice in toward the offlying bar. Occasionally we could see the ice, but mainly we heard it groaning and crashing, as the blocks grated together all night.

Day 73: August 16

The wind subsided and we awoke to find a sheen of ice on the tent and boat. This was the season's first morning ice, and yet another reminder that we needed to make miles before freeze-up. We set off at 5:00 am and paddled across open lagoon, admiring the Romanzof Mountains standing much closer to the coast than one might have expected. The peaks harbored fresh snow, and the highest ones were hidden in the clouds. The sky looked like it was about to clear, but a black cloud raced overhead, bringing winds at eight knots on our starboard quarter.

We were glad when we finally reached the first pass where we could slip out of the lagoon, and put the bar between the weather and us. To our pleasant surprise, the wind had not blown the pack ice tight against the outside of the bar. The pack stood a quarter mile off, and there it remained throughout the day. Unfortunately, the shore lead was often chock-a-block with shore-fast floes, and we spent the day weaving among them, often wondering if we would be able to get through. From any distance they often looked closed-in.

The bar fronting Beaufort Lagoon was very low lying - two feet high at most. But beyond Siku Entrance, the Icy Reef was quite high - six feet - and would have made good camping for most of its length.

While paddling among these unending floes, we decided to christen the boat "Siku Kayak." In the Eskimo language, the word siku means "sea ice," and to us it seemed a fitting name for this kayak which seemed so at home in these ice-strewn waters.

Mid-morning a barge went chugging past, heading east. Farther along we would see it again on the east side of Demarcation Bay, where its crew was dismantling a station of some sort.

Lying on one of the many thousands of floes was a pod of six seals. Their dark, glossy bodies were like silhouettes against the white ice. While some rested, others kept watch. A small head with a pointed snout bobbed in the water nearby, turning one way, then the other, watching for approaching danger and smelling the air for intruders. These creatures were extremely wary, and reminded us, too, to be on the lookout for polar bears.

After crossing the mouth of Demarcation Bay we landed on a bar and discovered another crossing ahead. We seemed to be on an island instead. This was our first rest in 27 miles, and we were deeply chilled. So we built a fire, and as usual this had a wonderfully warming effect, as did the steaming cuppas and hot pancakes with butter and syrup. As an experiment

Siku Kayak -- 229

I placed a couple of softball-sized rocks in the fire. Extracting them ten minutes later, I let them cool just enough to handle, then wrapped them in bandannas and placed one in each cockpit. The heat kept our feet and legs warm for nearly an hour.

Now in total calm we made our way along the mainland coast, which soon became a long series of 30-foot high mud bluffs. Finally we came to a large antenna delineating the border between the US and Canada. We landed ashore and climbed the bank, then walked 50 yards across marshy tundra to a stubby pillar known as "Monument 1." This was the initial marker in a long series that followed the border south.

The farther we progressed, the larger and more closely packed were the floes. People of Kaktovik had said the ice was unusually heavy for this time of year. One fellow said that in the 30 years he had lived there, he had seen only two other summers where the ice had not moved off.

The floes were so unstable that dragging the boat over them was not an option. Typically they were undercut around their edges by as much as six feet, and were continually collapsing or rolling over. We could only weave among them, occasionally elbowing our way between massive pieces. Our biggest challenge was in reaching shore, now fronted in smaller but much more tightly packed chunks. Usually we had to search for a semi-open lead, then shove the remaining blocks aside to gain access to the beach.

230 -- *Siku Kayak*

At the first possible campsite, what did we find but huge bear tracks. Continuing another 45 minutes until dark clouds began threatening imminent rain, we stopped at 6:00 pm at a gash in the cutbank. Here we found no bear tracks in evidence, but we did notice a freshly torn up ground squirrel den.

Before carrying the boat to camp, we always unloaded the gear from its forward and aft compartments, in order to lessen the boat's weight. But it was still enormously heavy with its central locker full of food. This food was not bagged and would have taken a while to unload. So as we struggled up the slope, through the gash, and across uneven tundra to our intended campsite, we pondered the possibility that we might have overdone it in the groceries department, over-reacting to the previous leg's famine. But at the same time we knew that a large supply might be essential if we were stopped by the pack ice.

Day's Run: 40 n-mi, 13 hrs. Camp: 69° 38.301' N, 140° 56.085' W

Day 74: August 17

Stormbound in a northwesterly, we remained in the tent all day, forlornly watching the ice floes marching past like exhibits in a parade. Each floe had its own identity, size, and color, and many were shaped in bizarre ways – mainly from the effects of occasional upturning to differing angles. We could not understand why the wind was not packing the floes tight against shore, but was merely sweeping them past, parallel to shore.

In the day's continual rain we tried to read our books, but could not concentrate very well, due to the anxiety factor. We were not real sure that proceeding ahead was the right thing to do. The season was getting late; the temperatures were dropping, and the storms were becoming more frequent. The presence of the floes added an otherworldly dimension, and a very wintry one at that. We hoped that beyond Herschel Island we would find open water in the somewhat warmer temperatures of the great Mackenzie River delta. Another week's worth of good days would put us there, but the good days were getting harder to come by.

Day 75: August 18

We arose at 4:00 am to the sound of the little creek gurgling nearby. Since we could hear the creek, that meant the wind had ceased. Carrying Siku to water's edge was as strenuous as ever.

We set off at 5:30 am, not quite sure how we were going to negotiate the tightly packed floes ahead. Somehow a way always opened, although it often required considerable zigzagging. At least the floes were a blessing in one regard: a northeast wind started to blow, and the ice kept the seas down. Often I would steer into the wake of a large floe and we would paddle in its lee. The air temperature was well below freezing, as indicated by the ice accumulating in my beard and on Jenny's spray skirt. The fog was thick and we were a bit worried about the possibility of encountering a polar bear.

The shotgun was stored in a homemade waterproof neoprene case, and stowed in a specially built rack under the starboard deck in my cockpit. This rack had a quick-release for ease of access. But mainly because of the waterproof case, the access was not instant. We would use the gun only as a last resort, but neither would we ever go to the Arctic coast without it.

232 -- *Siku Kayak*

By 8:00 am the wind had grown strong enough to persuade us to head for shore. Where the banks had been high mud, here was a low spot, so we landed at a beautiful creek coursing into the sea. A number of muskox tracks were imprinted in the clay, along with a set of bear tracks. We pitched the tent on the wet clay and gravel, because the more insulating tundra was lacking. Inside the tent we warmed ourselves with extra clothes and the sleeping quilt.

Jenny wandered down to the creek to filter drinking water, then went for a short walk, staying within sight of the tent. The region had a certain rawness, as though just yesterday a massive ice sheet had retreated and left it exposed. The ground was drier than the boggy tundra we had so often seen. There were no rusting oil drums or any other sign of human visits, and despite the wind and mist, a hush covered the pristine land. Inland, the terrain sloped gently up to meet the British Mountains. The scud lifted enough to show some of them glistening in fresh snow. The creek was an excellent source of water, among the best of the summer. We slept until the wind calmed and the rain stopped, about 12:30 pm.

August 18, midday stop, 2½ hrs. Camp: 69° 36.296' N, 140° 37.938'W

August 18 continued

Setting off at 1:15 pm, we dodged in and out among the sometimes densely packed floes, a few times backtracking out of one cul de sac or another. These floes were obviously blown in by yesterday's wind. The coast here was gradually concave and acted like a catch basin. The farther we went, the larger the floes, and with them the larger the anxiety factor. The wind piped up and rain started pummeling down. A DEW Line Station came into view, and gave us something of an immediate goal. Here again the coastline was mostly high mud bank, with lower sections widely spaced where various creeks had cut through.

Jenny spotted a muskox on the top of a cutbank. It stood there placidly, watching us paddle past. The sight of an animal was somehow assuring, especially one so well adapted. It made the region seem less hostile.

Reaching the Komakuk Beach DEW station, we found it to be operational, as evidenced by a few lights and the sound of a generator. This was the first station we had seen with its original radar reflectors still standing. The sight of the buildings seemed to make our plight all the more grim, because the temptation to stop was great. Showers would have been nice, as well as a bear-free place to sleep. But we knew that this would only weaken us, and besides, we had no desire to carry the kayak the quarter-mile inland.

A short ways past the station we landed at what looked like an Inupiaq campsite on high gravel and sand. A huge set of bear tracks coursed through, going both ways. These dissuaded us from camping. But mainly we wanted to cook a meal. So at the water's edge we lit the stove and quickly pan-fried a couple of juicy steaks. Despite our preponderance of food, we had not been eating well, due to the very limited cooking opportunities, and to our reduced appetites from the stress associated with the pack ice. While cooking, we both hunkered around the stove for its scant warmth. The contrast between the harsh world of the ice floes, frigid air, and polar bears, and the secure housing of the nearby DEW station was almost unbearable. But the steaks tasted divine and made us feel much better.

We pressed on, weaving in and out amongst the floes, and wearing our sou'westers in the pattering rain. My neoprene mittens had served me well all summer, but were no longer adequate in these frigid temperatures. So for the first time I wore shell mitts over two thick fleece liners – all home-made - and these worked well. I suggested to Jenny that we paddle another mile, but she wanted to paddle another hour. That suited me even better, and again I was thankful for a partner with equal determination.

Eventually the shoreline began to lower, and we decided we had better stop while the stopping was good. So we found a way through the shorefast floes and landed ashore. Slogging across the loose gravel up a wide, sloped beach, at 6:30 pm we made camp among a cluster of driftwood

Siku Kayak -- 235

Finding our way among the floes is becoming more difficult.

logs. Grizzly tracks led every which way; at least we hoped they were grizzly and not Nanook.

We pitched the tent just as the rain began, and as a precaution set a number of poles behind the tent as a barricade of sorts, or at least a bit of warning should bruin wander too close from that direction. The kayak's starboard rudder cord had frayed nearly all the way through, at the pulley, of all places. So I removed the line and fitted a new one. Then I joined Jenny inside our warm and comfy abode.

While loading and unloading in the rain, the outsides of our drybags became soaked. These were store-bought bags of the type used for river rafting, and were coated only on the insides. This arrangement left the outside fabric to absorb water. They needed to be coated on the outsides so that we could have simply wiped them dry.

Day's Run: 21 n-mi, 7¾ hrs. Camp: 69° 36.675' N, 139° 59.905' W

The kayak covered in snow.

Day 76: August 19

For the initial half of the night, rain fell hard and steady. But when the drumming on the tent ceased, we knew the rain had turned to snow. In the morning we peered out the doorway and found three inches carpeting the landscape. Everything was Arctic white except for a few small patches of open water that was more like an unwelcoming steel grey. The kayak looked out of its element covered in snow and plastered along its sides with frozen rain. Not wishing to face the inevitable quite yet, I pulled the quilt back over my head.

"There's a bear outside!" Jenny warned. I sprung to my knees, grabbed the shotgun and snapped its action closed, and poked its muzzle out the open doorway - just in time to see the obese back end of a huge grizzly

Grizzly bear #24 paid a visit to this camp. The huge tracks lead right to the kayak.

rushing away. It ran maybe 300 yards across open tundra towards the mountains, then slowed to a purposeful gait and kept right on going. For several minutes we watched it grow smaller and smaller, until finally it vanished in the vastness.

I went outside for a look at the tracks, and found each print as long as my own foot but much wider. "Big Foot" had been ambling along the beach in our direction, apparently not noticing us. But twenty feet away, it turned abruptly and walked to the bow of the kayak, which was just a few feet

The way ahead is becoming increasingly clogged with ice. We managed only another four miles beyond this camp.

from the tent. Whether it smelled us, or heard Jenny's voice or the snap of the shotgun's action, the bear suddenly bounded fearfully away, leaving deeply imprinted and widely-spaced tracks in the fresh snow and soft gravel.

The weather was starting to clear, so I pulled on my mukluks with their fleece liners and began to scrape the snow off the yak and tent. The sun came out intermittently, and dried the tent's sunny side, while leaving it frozen on its shady side. At Jenny's suggestion I turned the fly around. The wind had diminished, so we decided to set off. The only question was: which way?

As I packed, Jenny cooked eggs and sausage, then a couple of steaks for the road. With winter just around the corner, the weather was more frigid and the floes larger and more tightly packed. We felt a strong pull back to the DEW Line Station at Komakuk, from where we might be able to call for an air taxi. We debated the matter, but ultimately decided to proceed ahead with caution.

Carrying Siku to the water, we found that large areas had skimmed over with ice. This was more ominous news. Even though this skimming indicated the presence of salt-free water from the nearby river delta, we also realized that a more serious storm could freeze the entire sea's surface. Still, we figured we could at least walk back to the DEW Line Station. So again with trepidation, owing mainly to the density of floes, we decided to try pressing ahead.

Shoving off at 4:30 pm we wove among huge floes, mostly staying a quarter mile offshore in the widest openings. We managed three or four miles, and were within a mere 12½ miles of Herschel Island when we

Looking ahead at the ever thickening floes, this is
Nunaluk beach, our turn-around point.

both realized that the situation was starting to become a little too dangerous. We found a lead and turned for shore, and landed on the Nunaluk gravel bank.

Here we shared a conversation that lasted about a minute. We both sensed that we had reached our Rubicon, and judgment suggested we dare not cross it. Every now and then, one comes to a point of no return, and this was ours. As much as we dearly wanted to press on for Inuvik, we both knew that if we continued ahead much further, we might not survive.

We had traveled a challenging 100 miles from Kaktovik, but figured we only needed to backtrack to the DEW Line Station and call for an air taxi. Quite possibly we could leave the boat there for the winter with plans of returning the following summer. In only a few hours we could be whisked away to warmer climes. At least in theory. Disappointed, we turned around and began heading back.

Along the way we passed a seal resting on a floe. I whistled softly, and the seal put its head down on the floe, then raised it again. We repeated the game three or four more times. It must have sensed we were no threat, because it could have easily slid into the water.

Halfway to the station we heard the rumble of engines and saw three native skiffs hammering eastward. The people passed us a quarter mile out - close enough to exchange hearty waves. They were charging full tilt and were not about to stop, and we sensed great urgency in their plight, as in our own. We hoped they would manage to punch through and reach their village, probably Aklavik in the delta, we thought.

Paddling back toward Komakuk we made fairly good time. A quarter mile of fuel pipe road led to the complex, from which came the dull roar of a big generator. Boot prints and tractor tracks on this road appeared to be a few days old. But reaching the station we were dismayed to find no fresh tracks around the buildings. Moreover, all the doors were locked -

save for those of a small bunkhouse. Search as we did, we could find no one.

We had seduced ourselves with the prospects of an easy out. But such was not to be, so we resolved to paddle the 20 miles back to Demarcation Bay, and see if the barge might still be there. Perhaps we could use its

The expanse of pristine coastline, the beauty of the sparkling sea and its ice floes, the tundra adorned in its fall colors and the mountains glistening with fresh snow - all were truly awesome.

radio to call for an air taxi, and the barge itself to transport the kayak to Kaktovik or Prudhoe.

In fading daylight we paddled several more miles, then headed for shore to check our location in relation to the lagoon behind the bar. In the process we had to break through a few areas of frozen sea.

On our way again, the cold-induced fatigue and fading light was making it difficult to avoid the clear-ice growlers. If the kayak collided with one of those it might capsize.

Reaching the area of our previous camp, we found that the small, unnamed river had swept the ice out of the way. This made for an easy route to shore, and we hoped and equally easy departure in the morning, should the margins of the sea freeze even more during the night. We landed at 9:30 pm, thankful to be on land despite the fresh bear tracks running this way and that.

During our trip we had not taken the trouble to leave our itinerary and contingency plans with a responsible party at each village. Now we were beginning to realize the error of this. Should problems arise, our absence could go unnoticed for a long while. Having been in this particular region more than a week now, we had not seen or heard a single airplane. So much for the usefulness of our hand-held VHF aircraft radio. Just being here was fairly risky, due to the opportunistic bears, the freezing temperatures, and most prominently the pack ice that was inexorably closing towards shore. We carried an old style class-B EPIRB, but would have been very reluctant to use it, and even then it guaranteed us nothing. More than any other time during the journey, we felt cut off from the world. But we realized, also, that it had been our desire and decision to carry on past Kaktovik, and it was now up to us to get ourselves back.

Day's Run: 15 n-mi, 5 hrs. Camp: 69° 36.296' N, 140° 37.938' W

Day 77: August 20

We awoke to a morning so frigid that ice plastered the yak. The wind was strong northeast and its chill factor well below zero. Moiling clouds stopped short of the ground, and away to the south were the flanks of the Romanzof Mountains, now glistening white with snow. Carrying the boat to water's edge, we were glad to find that the sea had not refrozen, probably because the wind had kept its surface in motion. As we were returning from the first load, the tent suddenly took flight, never mind the heavy rifle, grab-it-and-run bag, and a clothing bag inside. We had thought the weight of these items was sufficient to hold down the tent. Not so. We dashed to its rescue, and were greatly relieved to find nothing broken. This seemed a miracle when I found the rifle lodged behind one of the poles.

Without further incident we dismantled the tent, stowed its components in their proper bags, finished loading, and shoved off at 7:30 am.

The paddling was brisk to say the very least. As we grappled ahead in near gale conditions, the floes offered some protection from the wind, and in most cases were flattening the seas. The morning was so cold that spray was freezing on deck, and icicles were forming on Jenny's drysuit beneath her arms and elbows - and probably mine also. The wind had driven the pack ice harder ashore, and this required us to keep a full hundred yards out. Contrary to a few days ago, the ice was now much more compact and afforded very few opportunities of landing.

These floes were huge, but even so they could not be walked on or even stepped on, due to their instability. Ninety percent of such ice lies beneath the water's surface, so that when a floe rolls over it can pose a serious risk to anyone or anything near it. What causes them to roll over is the differential rate of melting above the water and below. And this melting was greatest this time of year.

We paddled briskly trying to stay warm, thankful that the wind was at our backs.

For the past couple of days we had been seeing great flocks of geese and ducks winging overhead in long wedges. The call of the wild goose heralds the end of the season, and must not be denied. To confuse the issue however, we were still seeing Oldsquaw ducks with young, or at least juveniles. Also, we enjoyed watching the juvenile gulls with their parents. The adults would swoop, dive and screech at us unmercifully while the juveniles merely flew around completely mystified by the ruckus. We were also seeing another pretty gull, possibly the mew gull, with red-orange feet, yellow bill, and grey wing tops and white underbelly. This one liked to perch on the ice.

In the vicinity of the Canada/Alaska border we were paddling among thickly clustered floes when we noticed that one of the smaller chunks was moving at about our same speed. A quick double-take and we realized it was a polar bear swimming in the icy water. For a few moments it hurried diagonally away from us. But when at a "safe" distance of about 100 feet, it reconsidered and began paralleling us, turning its mammoth head frequently to gauge our speed. With the distinct feeling it was testing us, we resisted the urge to bolt away, for fear that might trigger the animal's chase instincts. So we continued at our usual pace of about four knots, and after what seemed like eternity the huge beast lost interest and turned away.

Eventually we reached Demarcation Bay, where we had hoped to find the barge. But what we found instead was only more emptiness. The barge had gone, taking the crew and all their equipment with it.

This did not disappoint us like yesterday's incident at Komakuk, for we had learned not to place our hopes on any services that only "might" have been available. As we had suspected all morning, our task was now to paddle the remaining 60 miles to Barter Island. This was no longer a mere jaunt to be taken lightly. Quite possibly our survival depended on our ability to find a way through the ever-thickening floes.

Paddling across the bay's entrance was a bit dicey because we could not see the far side, and in this particular area the ice was minimal, leaving Siku wallowing in the following seas. Eventually we closed the far spit, and now paddling in a more northerly direction were taking the waves on the quarter, sometimes abeam.

Based on the weather trends of late, we knew that blue sky was more like an anomaly in the local meteorological patterns, and one that the Arctic tried to correct. A showing of blue did not mean that the sky was clearing. It was more like a hole in the water that would quickly fill. Nevertheless, we enjoyed a few heartening moments of sky, and even a bit of gleaming sunshine that melted the deck ice. But then, snow came slanting down, prompting us to pick up the pace in an attempt to maintain what precious body warmth was ours. Despite our struggles to preserve warmth, we seemed to be losing ground.

Midway along Icy Reef we found a rare lead heading toward shore, and spent five minutes pushing, pulling, and squeezing the yak through the final shore-bound floes. We landed safely, but about all we could do here was walk around, trying to warm up. The wind was blowing too strongly for a fire. We could have built a small wind block, but more than anything else, what we needed right now was miles. So we forced the boat back out through the ice and continued on our way.

In another four miles we had gone about as far as we could this side of genuine hypothermia. So we started looking for another channel toward shore. We found one that went nearly there, but even so, Jenny had to climb from her cockpit and crawl onto the bow, and for ten minutes shove the floes sluggishly away. Even twenty feet from shore, the water was too deep to wade. Ever so slowly, with the floes parting begrudgingly, we nosed Siku in. The time was 2:30 pm.

We trudged up a sloped gravel bank, which here was about six feet high, and selected a place to camp. While pitching the tent we were hit with a blizzard of snow. This snow we had to shake off the tent before fitting its fly. The sun came out for a few fleeting moments, long enough to melt the snow before losing itself to the clouds again, and leaving us in the frigid blast. "Thank goodness for this tent," we uttered as we crawled inside. It was so secure and protective, and we could not have managed the trip without it. It was heavy and difficult to pitch, but well worth it.

I mopped the tent's interior, while outside Jenny organized the food and collected a few small logs on which to cook. This was our first camp with no bear tracks of late, although we certainly did not discount the possibility, especially since the main body of the polar pack reached to within half a mile of shore.

Preparing for bed had become a lengthy process. Typically, Jenny changed into her dry nightshirt, and put her dank paddling shirt over that to help dry it. Still wearing her sweat-soaked pants, she put two pairs of dry pants over them. After donning parka and balaclava, she removed her socks and tucked them into the waistband of her pants, where her body heat would help dry them. She then put on two pair of dry wool socks. For some reason I rarely sweat-soaked my paddling clothes, so I simply donned my parka over them, changed into dry socks and stowed my paddling socks in my waistband for drying.

Jenny reached outside the doorway where she had left the stove heating a pot of water, and brought the pot it in to fill our water bottles. These we placed at our feet for warmth and to help dry the dank quilt. We drank hot lemonades, cider, soup, and ate a few snacks, then fell into a sleep so sound that it more resembled suspended animation.

Day's Run: 28 n-mi, 7 hrs. Camp: 69° 46.564' N, 141° 39.879' W

The land was now white. The shore-fast floes sometimes extended half-a-mile offshore, and just beyond that was the polar pack ice itself. But more disconcerting, the sea was starting to freeze around the shore-fast bergs, as seen in this photo.

Winter is fast approaching and the sea is beginning to freeze. Here we are cutting through a half-inch layer of salt-free surface ice, while pushing and shoving our way out to an open lead.

Day 78: August 21

Leaving camp at 7:00 am, we forced our way back out through the shore-fast floes and into somewhat open water. The conditions were similar to those of yesterday, with floes so compact that they kept us well out from shore – now several hundred yards at least. We were reasonably confident

A fine day for sea-kayaking, not counting the ice forming in the shadow under Jenny's right arm.

we could make it back to Kaktovik, but knew it would be a challenge. At least today's wind was fairly light, even if the air was cold. As we labored ahead for mile after mile, I again watched the ice accumulating beneath the elbows and forearms of Jenny's drysuit.

The farther we progressed toward Kaktovik, the thicker the ice and the farther from shore it drove us. On and on we went, through the afternoon while looking for an opening that would enable us to reach shore. One time we managed to land for an extremely cold pit stop, and later to hastily fry a steak.

Four days and 90 miles after turning back, Kaktovik is only ten more miles ahead.

We had hoped to paddle into the far extension of Jago Lagoon just beyond Griffin Point, but the floes were so pervasive that we could not find the pass, let alone paddle through it. We were starting to grow concerned, because the openings toward shore were practically non-existent, and no longer could we shove away the floes in order to reach land. They were too compact, and would not budge. We debated returning a couple miles back to a place where we thought we could get to shore, but Jenny was more in favor of continuing ahead, in hopes that we would find a better route to shore.

And so we pressed on, following a narrow lead that gradually angled ever farther away from shore. Improbable though it seemed, at last we came to an open slot that led a quarter mile towards shore. Shoving the

Looking towards shore a quarter mile away.

few remaining car-sized chunks aside, with enormous relief we landed on the beach.

The time was 6:30 pm, and to our surprise we found that we had landed near our picnic site with Daniel and Lillian. In fact, we even noticed tracks of our shoes and boots.

We set up camp and lay the frozen drysuits and other gear on the driftwood to dry as much as possible. Then we built a cheery campfire to warm ourselves, and to dry socks, shirts and mittens. Our homemade overmitts had been leaking at the seams, and Jenny had worn hers so much that the coating itself was gone from the palms. So while paddling in wind-driven seas, our hands had been continually wet, as were the fleece mittens worn inside the overmitts.

The fire cheered our spirits, and we decided to ignore the bear danger and cook a reviving meal. Despite the freezing temperatures, this was our most comfortable camp in several weeks, thanks to the warming fire and hot meal. And with the open lagoon now before us, the pressure was off. We were confident in making Kaktovik the following morning.

Day's Run: 36 n-mi, 11½ hrs. Camp: 70° 05.772 N, 143° 01.649' W

Day 79: August 22

Portaging kayak and gear across the sandbar, we shoved off into the ice-free lagoon. The winds were from ahead but light, and within a few hours we could make out the radar domes at Kaktovik. Air taxis were coming and going, and soon we could see the airport buildings. But near the village whalebone pile we ran into trouble.

Three people were shooting rifles out across the water, unfortunately in our direction. Evidently they had failed to notice us this far out. We certainly noticed them, with explosions visible from their rifles, and a few of their bullets whizzing past frighteningly close. I fired off a shotgun round, which momentarily deafened us, but at least had desired effect; the people stopped shooting and withdrew from the beach.

Paddling around the backside of the airport buildings, we landed ashore mid-morning. This seemed like the most convenient place to prepare for the flight home, and to ready Siku for her trip south. So here we made camp, then walked into town for laundry and showers. And of course we surprised Daniel and Lillian by stopping at their house to say hello.

Jenny arranged the kayak's shipment, and booked a flight for ourselves to Fairbanks. I removed Siku's rudder, while Jenny emptied the compartments. Into these we stowed some of the lighter, more bulky gear, such as the quilt, foam pads, life jackets, and seat cushions. Then we wrapped the entire boat with plastic sheeting and used a roll of tape to secure the plastic in place.

Day's Run: 15 n-mi, 5 hrs. Camp: 70° 08.004' N, 143° 37.079' W

Back at Kaktovik, another fabulous adventure comes to a close.

August 23

The airplane was loading when Daniel and Lillian stopped by on their 4-wheeler to see us off. Saying good-bye to our friends, we boarded the small plane, and soon were enjoying spectacular views of the ice-choked Beaufort Sea below. Flying over the rugged and snow-covered Brooks Range was another rare spectacle. The cabin heater was on high, so we started shedding outer garments one after another, until we had completely filed a nearby seat. Other passengers did the same. The contrast between the pilot in shirtsleeves and our mountain of shed garments made us realize just how much clothing we had been wearing.

The trip had been a fabulous adventure - everything we had hoped for and a great deal more. In those 79 days we had explored a huge expanse of coastal wilderness, pristine and largely untouched. Altogether we had spotted 24 grizzlies and one polar bear, a dozen muskox, thousands of caribou and countless birds, several types of seals and four species of whales.

We had not achieved our objective of reaching Tuktoyuktuk or Inuvik. Close but not quite. Still, we felt we had given it our best, and that in return, the Arctic had given us its best. The experiences had been unparalleled, and we felt privileged and fortunate to have accomplished what we had. Turning back at Nunaluk had been very disappointing, of course. The line had presented itself and fate had dared us to cross it. But we felt we had decided correctly. All through history, overly-focused adventures have perished in their struggles to succeed. Always the result of crossing the line, always when the person allowed the goal to become master.

Siku Kayak had proven her true worth, and we were particularly gratified in having designed and built her ourselves. Already I had several ideas for an improved version, for our next trip. We had even named this future kayak "Nunaluk." This was the beach where the pack ice had turned Siku back. And we hoped it would be the starting point for this new boat, come next summer.

By the time our flight reached Oregon we were beginning to thaw. But when we stepped off the plane we practically melted. How ironic that the region was undergoing a heat wave, with temperatures nearly in the 100's. But ice cubes in our lemonade? No thanks.

Author's Profile

Ray Jardine holds a degree in Aeronautical and Astronautical Engineering from Northrop University. He worked in the aerospace industry as a specialist in computer-simulated space-flight mechanics, but retired at an early age to pursue his outdoor interests.

Ray climbed most of Colorado's fourteeners, many in winter. He has also climbed extensively across western North America. His highest peak was Peru's Huascarán, at 22,205 feet.

A wilderness instructor, Ray worked for the Colorado Alpine Winter Mountaineering School for two seasons, and Outward Bound for seven. During these classes he accumulated several thousand backpacking miles. He also holds an EMT certificate from St. Anthony's Hospital in Denver.

A rock climber for 19 years, Ray established some of the era's toughest climbs, including the world's first 5.12 graded climb, The Crimson Cringe, and the first 5.13, The Phoenix. He climbed extensively in Great Britain and across western America. His ascents in Colorado include seven Diamond routes. In Yosemite Valley he pioneered 50 first ascents, and was the first to free climb a grade VI. He invented the protection and anchoring device known as the "Friend," which revolutionized the sport. And he originated the style of climbing used today that enables far more challenging routes to be climbed. According to Rock & Ice magazine, "The brilliance of his routes, the undeniable contributions of his designs, and his yet-unrealized visions of the future of the sport place Ray Jardine among the rarest of climbing revolutionaries."

Retiring from climbing in the early 1980's, Ray with his wife Jenny put to sea aboard their ketch SUKA, acronym for "Seeking UnKnown Adventures," and sailed around the world in 3½ years. Ray is also a PADI-certified scuba diver.

Ray has flown sailplanes, and has an Australian Restricted Private Pilot's License. He is also an avid hang glider pilot, having logged some 400 hours aloft, flown to 16,000 feet, cross-country 50 miles, and thermal gained 9,100 feet (nearly two miles straight up).

In 1987 the Jardines hiked from Mexico to Canada, generally along the Pacific Crest Trail. In 1991 they hiked the PCT again. In 1992 they hiked the Continental Divide Trail, in 1993, the Appalachian Trail, and in 1994 they hiked the PCT southbound. Experienced gleaned from these trips inspired Ray to write two books about long-distance hiking: *The Pacific Crest Trail Hiker's Handbook* (out of print) and *Beyond Backpacking*.

In 1999, Ray and Jenny were featured guests in the BBC television series *Wilderness Walks* with host Cameron McNeish.

Together, Ray and Jenny have sea-kayaked several thousand miles in areas such as offshore California, the Sea of Cortez, French Polynesia, Australia, Alaska and Canada. In 1988 they paddled from Anacortes, Washington 3,300 miles through the Inside Passage, over the Chilkoot trail by portage, and down the Yukon River to the Bering Sea. Continuing the summer of 1995 in a kayak of their own design and construction, they paddled another 600 miles along the rugged coast of Arctic Alaska. And the summer of 1996 they returned in yet another home-built kayak and paddled the remaining 1,400 miles to Point Barrow and across the top of Alaska and a ways into Canada – as described in this book. In 1997 they built another kayak, "Nunaluk" and paddled it 975 miles down the Mackenzie River, then 200 miles of Arctic coastline until stopped by polar pack ice at Tuktoyuktuk. That same summer they paddled a canoe 575 miles down the remote Thelon River from Lynx Lake to the Inuit hamlet of Baker Lake near Hudson Bay. Subsequent canoe trips across the Barrenlands of Arctic Canada have included the Back and Meadowbank Rivers, 730 miles, and the Kazan River, 560 miles.

Avid skydivers specializing in free-flying, Ray has made 2,600 jumps and Jenny 2,000.

The fall of 2002, the Jardines rowed their 23-foot ocean rowboat "Caper" across the Atlantic Ocean. Powered by oars alone, they made the 3,000-mile crossing in 53 days.

The summer of 2003 they created the IUA Hike & Bike, a Canada to Mexico trip of 2,000 miles. And in 2004 they peddled a tandem bicycle 6,700 miles coast-to-coast, round-trip from their home.

For more information about the Jardines, their stories, books, videos, kits and classes, visit Ray's web site at www.RayJardine.com or search for "Ray Jardine's Adventure Page".

Siku Kayak (left) and her successor Nunaluk

Ray-Way Products

www.RayJardine.com

P.O. Box 2153, Arizona City, AZ 85223

We invite you to visit our web site for more information about our products:

Beyond Backpacking

First published in 1998, this book is now in its fourth printing and continues to be the leading source of information on lightweight hiking and backpacking. Written by Ray Jardine. Published by AdventureLore Press. ISBN 0-9632359-3-1

The Ray-Way Tarp Book

The how's and why's of camping comfortably beneath a ray-way tarp instead of in a tent. Detailed instructions on use, and making one yourself at home. Instructions also for the net-tent, stowbags, and PolyTarp. Written by Ray Jardine. Published by AdventureLore Press. ISBN 0-9632359-5-8

Atlantic Caper, the video

A fantastic, 48 minute glimpse into the world of ocean rowing, this video chronicles Ray and Jenny's 3,000 mile Atlantic crossing. From sea trials, training and gear preparations to the boat's launching, provisioning and departure day, this presentation shows what it takes to make a trip of this magnitude become reality. The actual footage at sea, the mid-ocean close-encounters with freighters, the sometimes rough motion, the rolling, flying spray, calm sunsets... will put you there on the rower's seat.

This video captures the determination and thrill of crossing an ocean in a small rowboat, and the joy of a successful landfall after 53 days. Produced by Ray Jardine, 2003. Available in VHS and DVD.

Ray-Way Kits

These kits mark the beginning of the ray-way line of sew-your-own outdoor gear and clothing. They contain all the materials needed, along with step-by-step sewing instructions. Check www.rayjardine.com for prices and additional kits as they become available.